God's Girls

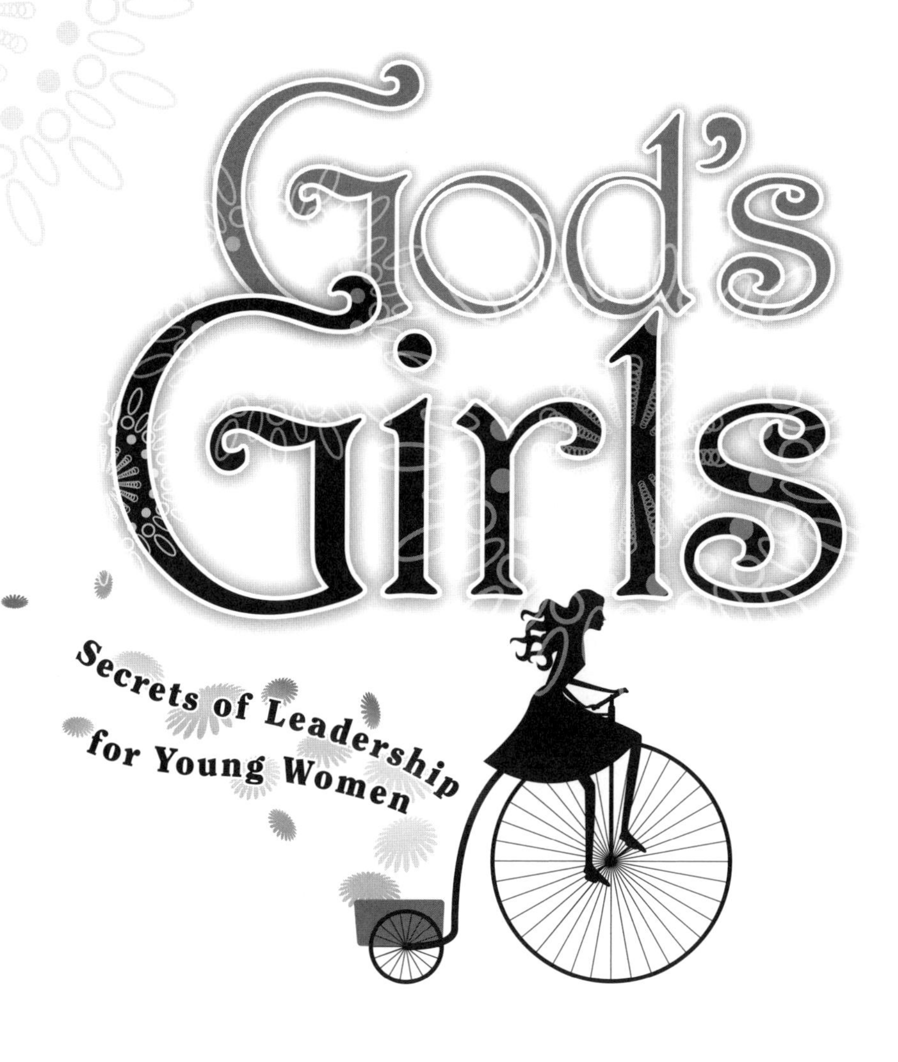

God's Girls

Secrets of Leadership for Young Women

Teresa Hampton

Publishing Designs, Inc.

Publishing Designs, Inc.
P.O. Box 3241
Huntsville, Alabama 35810

Second Printing 2015

Edited by Peggy Coulter

Printed in the United States of America

Publisher's Cataloging-in-Publication Data

Hampton, Teresa
God's girls / Teresa Hampton; foreword by Brenda Johnson
158 pp.
Thirteen chapters—Daily Devotions—Side-text questions.
1. Teenage girls—Religious life—Leadership. 2. Young women—Religious life—Leadership
ISBN 978-0-929540-79-5

248.8'33—dc22

Dedication

To the girls—now adults—that
I've had the privilege of teaching,
especially Jill, Charlotte, Laura, and
Morgen, who patiently answered my
questions and guided me to a better
understanding of the great strength
within each young person.

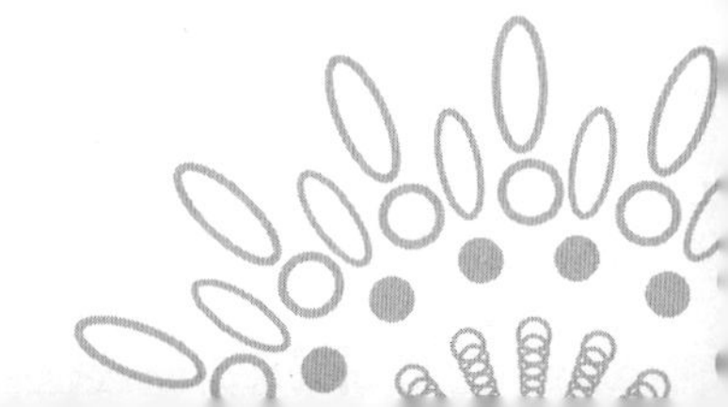

Contents

Foreword

Is there anything as precious as young, innocent girls? They always make me smile because they transport me to the time when I was young and eager to please God. How important, then, is it to teach them to become God's girls? It is vital to the Lord's body and to the world, although the world doesn't seem to understand it. Women hold the keys to the home and they strengthen the church because of their God-given role to nurture and teach their children. A godly mother wields her good influence on her children until her death. How do we insure that the church is filled with godly mothers? We blaze the trail by training our girls to be God's girls.

Many of the woes in our sinful world started with the demise of the home. Now a broken home is the norm. A woman on a reality television program said she "missed the various times when she had been a wife." Imagine that! She had been married so many times that her "homes" became blurred mixtures in her mind. Broken homes are not God's plan. The place to prevent domestic catastrophes is with the youth, before their lives are saturated with sin.

God's Girls is a beautiful biblical study we can use to teach our girls in the classroom or at home exactly how to live up to the name "Christian." Teresa's simple yet profound approach will touch and train young hearts who are poised to become women of God. Most important, *God's Girls* zeroes in to train "tomorrow's women" to be leaders! This leadership is not defined by the success-standard of the world, but by God—girls leading through service. They in turn will train the young women of the future.

Teresa has a great understanding of the issues facing girls in this modern world of sin. She doesn't shy away from encouraging them to challenge the culture by holding to God's unchanging hand. *God's Girls* defines a spiritual leader and gives practical, biblical advice on becoming one. I was particularly touched by Teresa's wisdom regarding dress, purity, and words.

In my opinion, this book covers the important matters that pertain to developing a well-rounded spiritual and physical life that glorifies the Lord! Any Christian girl who opens her Bible to the scriptures outlined on these pages will find herself on the inside track to leadership, God's way.

All God's girls should be given the opportunity to learn from this material. I am convinced that training them now for service in the kingdom will assure a bright and wonderful future for our Lord's church as they grow into God's women!

Brenda Johnson
Lads to Leaders / Leaderettes

Introduction

"Will you teach the young women?" That question jolted me into the real world; my first emotion was terror. Over the course of the next six years, however, a dramatic role reversal transpired—I became the student and they became my teachers. What a treasure! My terror was transformed into joy.

Every day of my experience was unique. One day the girls would come to class emotionally high, giddy with laughter, and the next day they might be filled with solemn expressions or anger or tears. They were young adults one day, discussing adult ideas and wanting to be treated as such. But the following day they were as likely as not to reveal childlike expectations or behavior.

In a very short time I made an amazing discovery. Aside from their roller-coaster emotions, these girls were very much like me as they tried to find their place in the body of Christ. As spiritually motivated, blossoming young adults, they eagerly sought to know God's Word and to understand the adult female role in the home, the church, and the community.

I have since talked with many young women and discovered that whether in school, in college, or in the working world of singles, they are searching for their place in the church.

Are you seeking to know God better? Do you want to know more about how young women can best serve God in the twenty-first century? If so, embark with me on a fascinating journey as we explore our role as women of God.

God's Girls Understand True Leadership

Remember now your Creator in the days of your youth, before the difficult days come, and the years draw near when you say, I have no pleasure in them.

Ecclesiastes 12:1

Jan was a petite college freshman with long blonde hair and a soft voice. Her beautiful smile brightened any day, but she was different from all her friends—very different—and her difference was obvious. You see, Jan was born without arms and hands. Her feet and legs were also her hands and arms. With them she dressed, put on makeup, walked to class, turned pages, and took notes. And I might add, her makeup was flawless and her penmanship was beautiful. She drove anywhere she wanted to go in her personal, specially adapted car. In a special interview, the school newspaper reporter asked about plans for the future.

"My short-range goal is to finish my degree in social work. My long-range goal is to use that knowledge to work with those who have extreme challenges and obstacles in their lives.

The interviewer then asked, "Is there anything you have not tried and mastered?"

Jan replied in her soft, quiet voice, "I've had success with everything except roller skating. But I haven't given up on it."

What an example! What a leader! Jan often led both students and teachers to a greater faith and trust in God. She showed how to rise above mediocrity and realize the full potential to touch others for good. Yes, the school was impacted by her spiritual devotion, encouraged by her positive attitude, and influenced by her determination to live life to its fullest. Aren't these the things that make a leader?

My Influence

Write the word *influence* in each blank below. Then discuss why each sentence is true.

My choice of words has

________________________________.

My choice of entertainment has

________________________________.

My choice of friends has

________________________________.

Older & Wiser

Interview an adult. Ask one question: *What influenced you most positively in your teen years?* Compare answers in class.

Guide, Conduct, and Influence

A leader guides, conducts, or influences another. Obviously, every person, regardless of age or gender, influences others either positively or negatively. As Christians, we want to lead positively. We'll learn in the next chapter how God intends for men to assume the more visible leadership positions. Men are the spiritual leaders in the home, in the church, and in worship, but we women must never forget that we also lead others, many times in quiet but powerful ways. We will begin to understand true leadership by asking a few questions.

* *Must a leader be physically attractive?* No! The world has trapped us into believing beauty is everything. God's people, the Israelites, fell into the same trap. Neighboring countries had kings, but Israel had an old judge, Samuel. *A strong young king is just what we need*, they thought, *to compete in the world*. Samuel warned them of the pitfalls of having a king (1 Samuel 8:9–18).

Despite Samuel's warnings, the people were relentless in their desire to keep up with their neighbors. God gave them what they wanted—a mighty man: powerful, tall, handsome. *He will be a perfect king,* they thought.

What a disappointment. Almost immediately Saul began to disobey God. When he failed to destroy the Amalekites, God rejected Saul and asked the prophet to anoint a second king.

At last Samuel narrowed his search to the sons of Jesse. Arriving at Jesse's

Fair to Look On

Abram said to Sarai:
You are a woman of beautiful countenance. When the Egyptians see you, they will say, "This is his wife"; and they will kill me . . . Please say you are my sister . . . (Gen. 12:11).

Read Genesis 12:10–20. Was Sarai's beauty a negative or a positive factor? What happened as a result of her outward appearance?

Tall & Handsome

Do not look at his appearance or at his physical stature . . . the Lord does not see as man sees; for man looks at the outward appearance, but the Lord looks at the heart (1 Sam. 16:7).

My Heart Check-up

1. What do I treasure? (That's where my heart is—Matt. 6:21.)

____

____

2. How do I honor God? (Is my heart far from God?—Matt. 15:8.)

____

____

3. What am I thinking? (I am what I think—Prov. 23:7.)

____

____

Whatever

Whatever things are true,
whatever things are noble,
whatever things are just,
whatever things are pure,
whatever things are lovely,
whatever things are of good report

. . . ______________ _______

______________ ______________

(Phil. 4:8).

home, he was immediately convinced that Eliab, the oldest son, was God's choice. He looked like a king. He was of good stature—a good warrior he would be. "Surely the Lord's anointed is before him" (1 Samuel 16:6). Sorry, Samuel. You're wrong.

What had Samuel learned from his experience with King Saul, who seemed to be the perfect military and civil leader? He had learned nothing, so God intervened at Jesse's house:

> Do not look on his appearance or at the height of his stature, because I have refused him. For the Lord does not see as man sees; for man looks at the outward appearance, but the Lord looks at the heart (1 Samuel 16:7).

The same is true today. God is always more interested in the heart. If you have a heart that is willing to please God, you have the ability to lead others in a mighty way.

* *Must a leader have a great personality?* Absolutely not! Some say that even the most introverted individual will influence ten thousand during a lifetime.

Even with a quiet, shy nature, you can influence and guide others positively. Elizabeth did. When she learned in her old age she was going to give birth to baby John, she hid herself, not because she was ashamed but because she was joyful (Luke 1:24–25).

Quiet people have unique strengths. They are often good listeners and organizers. A quiet girl with a listening ear may prevent someone from acting in a rash, angry, or impulsive way. Her unassuming questions or humble advice may lead constructively.

Quiet people make great leaders *if they have willing hearts*.

Was She Shy?

And his sister stood afar off, to know what would be done to him. Then his sister said to Pharaoh's daughter, "Shall I go and call a nurse for you . . .?" And Pharaoh's daughter said to her, "Go." So the maiden went and called the child's mother (Exod. 2:4, 7–8).

Describe Miriam's personality. How did she save her baby brother Moses?

____

____

____

Faith or Fear?

God has not given us a spirit of fear, but of power and of love and of a sound mind (2 Tim. 1:7).

How is God bigger than my family?

____

____

____

How can my family discourage me?

Why must I fight in the Lord's army, regardless of what my family does?

Girl Leaves Family

Ruth left all her friends. She left her family. She left her country of Moab and moved to Bethlehem with her mother-in-law. Underline the phrase in the following scripture that shows that Ruth understood she was different from other girls.

You have comforted me, and have spoken kindly to your maidservant, though I am not like one of your maidservants (Ruth 2:13).

* *Must a leader have a strong Christian family?* No! Even if you live with an ungodly parent, you can still be a leader for Christ.

Remember Timothy, the young man Paul converted? His father was Greek and probably had little concern for spiritual matters. His temperament likely presented some difficult challenges for Timothy, but Timothy was a Christian first (Acts 16:1–2; 2 Timothy 1:5).

Your home may be one of many affected by divorce. You may have a stepmom or stepdad. Just remember that some Christian girls who live with both parents in a stable home have little encouragement because the parents do not share the passion of their daughter's faith.

No Christian has a right to give up, and that includes you. Who knows? You might lead your parents to Christ by providing a good example for them.

Girls, you can have a powerful impact on your families. Some of the most powerful leaders in the church are young women who, despite the odds, choose to serve God. God's girls practice true Christianity by actively teaching children, parents, and friends. They busy themselves assisting the ill and grief-stricken. They participate in local and foreign mission efforts. They assist young mothers during worship. Their good deeds are endless.

Having Christian parents makes Christian living easier, but it is not an essential ingredient. Young, single women have the ability to lead all ages in a sound direction.

* *Must a leader be of a particular age?* Absolutely not! You may believe you are not old enough or mature enough to lead others. Solomon disagrees. In his book of Ecclesiastes, he told young

My Impact for Service

Here are two ways I can practice Christianity this week:

1. ______________________________

____

2. ______________________________

____

Every Secret Thing

God will bring every work into judgment, including every secret thing, whether good or evil (Eccles. 12:14.)

How many of my works will God bring into judgment?

____

What "secret" things will be brought into judgment?

____

How does this verse motivate us to fear God and keep His commands?

____

____

Seize the Moment!

Remember now your Creator in the days of your youth (Eccles. 12:1).

List two ways to follow the previous command. (See Ecclesiastes 12:13.)

1. ______________________________

____

2. ______________________________

____

people to remember God in their youth.

Solomon knew there is no guarantee of tomorrow; but even if we had the assurance of tomorrow, we would need the spiritual foundation to help us learn to face adult responsibilities and hardships. "Seize the moment!"

Solomon says, essentially. "Don't wait until you reach adulthood to know the beauty and peace of serving God and drawing others near Him" (Ecclesiastes 12:1).

So what is a leader? She is a guide, a conductor, or an influence. A good leader does not have to be beautiful. She does not have to have an outgoing personality. She may be married or unmarried. She may have Christian or non-Christian parents. She doesn't have to be a certain age, because leadership is for those of any age. She doesn't have to be popular or wealthy. But there is one thing she must have if she is to be God's successful leader. *She must have a willing heart.*

As we continue this study, we will examine biblical examples of women and men who became great leaders despite obstacles. We will take a fresh look at female leadership. We will also remember God's list of a leader's traits, because the world chooses differently—the world chooses one who looks the part. We must remember that true leadership has emerged from a young shepherd boy and from a courageous young woman who, despite the challenge of an armless and handless body, leads by example. Willingness is a key ingredient.

Read the scripture in each line below. After each scripture, look in the mirror and ask yourself the question that follows it.

Day	Bible Reading	Self-Check
1	1 Samuel 16:7	Do I lead others in a positive direction?
2	Isaiah 53:2	Do I truly want to be like Jesus?
3	1 Peter 3:1–2	Do others observe my behavior and see Jesus?
4	Exodus 2:1–8	Do I obey God even during difficult situations?
5	2 Timothy 1:3–7	Do I listen to the counsel of wiser and older people?
6	Ecclesiastes 12:1	Do I remember God in my youth?
7	1 Samuel 17:33–37	Do I trust God to help me lead others?

CHAPTER 2

God's Girls Lead with Obedience

This is the love of God, that we keep His commandments. And His commandments are not burdensome.

1 John 5:3

How would you like to plant your feet on the rim of an active volcano? Exciting thought? Well, I did. On a trip to Hawaii, my husband Gary and I toured an active volcano area. Excited, we gravitated closer and closer to the crater. I was stunned by the steam vents hissing just ahead. I inched forward. The strong sulfuric odors burned my nostrils. My brain begged my feet to turn and run. Steam jets were but a few feet ahead of my toes. Then I saw the sign: STOP! I did just that. I didn't need a second warning. I wondered, *Do sane people actually ignore that sign and go past it?*

A few days later, we learned that a young photographer did ignore the sign in an attempt to film the great lava flow. He took one step too many and the ground gave way without warning. You know what happened to him? He, along with his camera, slid into the stream of flowing lava and vaporized. What a costly mistake!

Rules. The very sound of that word brings an instant rush of conflicting emotions. But what would our world be like without rules? "Great! Great!" is our initial response. Take time for contemplation and then move for a moment into a world with no rules. How does the traffic flow? How do people conduct themselves downtown—or anywhere else? What happens when your neighbor plants a tree in the middle of your driveway or invites his friends to a picnic in your backyard? Are you now ready to get out of your no-rules world? Of course you are. None of us want to go there, not for a minute.

Eat and Die!

The tree of life was also in the midst of the garden, and the tree of the knowledge of good and evil. Then the Lord God took the man and put him in the garden of Eden to tend and keep it. And the Lord God commanded the man, saying, "Of every tree of the garden you may freely eat; but of the tree of the knowledge of good and evil you shall not eat, for in the day that you eat of it you shall surely die" (Gen. 2:8–9; 15–17).

God told Adam the rules. Underline God's rule for Adam in the above Scripture.

God's Kids Broke the Rule

We don't like to admit it—perhaps we don't even realize it—but we seek boundaries, guidelines, and rules. Why? Because structure promotes an atmosphere of safety and assurance. Laws are for the good of society. Take a look at the home. Children need boundaries. Where there are no rules, security and love are lacking.

The Creator knew our special need, didn't He? He designed us to function best with rules. After making the beauties of heaven and earth, He created His kids, Adam and Eve (Genesis 2–3). He made the man first, forming him from dust, and placed him in Eden's beautiful garden paradise. But even within paradise, work had to be done and rules had to be kept. God told Adam to tend the garden and keep it. He also told him he could eat of any fruit in the garden, except the fruit from the tree of knowledge of good and evil. God made clear that a violation of that rule would bring death.

All the rules God made were simple—easy to understand. Adam explained God's laws to his newly formed wife; she understood them. We know she did because she recited every word about the forbidden fruit to the sly old serpent.

What would it have been like if Eve had refused to give in to Satan? We will never know, because she obeyed the serpent at her first opportunity instead of listening to God. Then she offered the fruit to Adam who was with her, and he made a wrong choice

Notice what Eve told the serpent:

And the woman said to the serpent, "We may eat the fruit of the trees of the garden; but of the fruit of the tree which is in the midst of the garden, God has said, 'You shall not eat it, nor shall you touch it, lest you die'" (Gen. 3:2–3).

1. Don't __________the fruit.

2. Don't __________the fruit.

What was the consequence of breaking the rules?

____

____

____

____

Did Eve understand the rules? How do we know?

____

____

____

____

____

____

God's Way or My Way?

How did the following people go against God to do it their way?

Moses (Num. 20:10–11)

Action ______________________

Consequence ______________________

____

Pharoah (Exod. 5:1–2)

Action ______________________

Consequence ______________________

____

Nadab & Abihu (Lev. 10:1–2).

Action ______________________

Consequence ______________________

____

Israelites – Golden Calf (Exod. 32:1–4)

Action ______________________

Consequence ______________________

____

Jonah (Jon. 1:1–3)

Action ______________________

Consequence ______________________

____

too. In fact, it appears that he had several choices. If he was in her presence when she ate the fruit—and it certainly appears he was—he could have prevented Eve from taking the fruit. At the very least, he could have chosen not to eat the fruit. Instead, he allowed her to sin and to lead him into sin, when he, the spiritual leader of the family, should have run that serpent off.

Up to their moment of disobedience, Adam and Eve had been as innocent as little children, shamelessly naked. When God came in the cool of the evening to walk with them, Adam and Eve were trying to hide because they were suddenly afraid because of their nakedness.

The world as they knew it had changed. They became engaged in a tug-of-war between good and evil; nothing would ever be the same. Their spiritual lives were forever changed; their relationship with God and each other were forever altered; their physical existence would be forever challenging.

Eve spent the rest of her life reaping the consequences of her pleasure-for-a-moment violation of God's will.

Oh, the serpent! He was the great deceiver. He made her do it! No way. Passing the buck doesn't work with God. It didn't then; it doesn't now. Breaking God's rules is always costly. God holds the violator responsible. He always has; He always will.

I don't want to be like Eve. Do you? Of course not! So when we study the vital roles that women of all ages have in the home, the church, and the community, we must stop and consider the importance of obedience—the importance of doing things God's way instead of our way.

Obedience and Submission

Obey and *submit* are very different words, but they mean the same thing. Obedience is submission; submission is obedience. Look at the

Ananias and Sapphira
(Acts 5:1–10)

Action ______________________________

Consequence ______________________________

____

Is Submit a Bad Word?

Submit: *verb* \səb-'mit\
1
a : to yield oneself to the authority or will of another : surrender; *b* : to permit oneself to be subjected to something <*submit* to surgery>
2
: to defer to or consent to abide by the opinion or authority of another

Circle the answer that best defines *submission*:

have to

get to

yield myself to

How does biblical submission involve my cooperation?

____

____

____

"I Have My Rights!"

Am I free as a Christian to please myself, or am I a slave to a master? Read Romans 6:16 and write your answer below.

Why must a slave be in submission?

Verses of Obedience

Ephesians 6:1—*Children obey your parents.*

Acts 5:29—*Obey God rather than men.*

Hebrews 13:17—*Obey those who rule over you, and be submissive.*

obedience/submission concept in the life of Jesus. He "became obedient to the point of death, even the death of the cross" (Philippians 2:8).

Jesus begged: "Father, if it is possible, let this cup pass from Me; nevertheless, not as I will, but as You will." Jesus, being perfect, did not want to have any relationship with sin, yet He knew His Father was going to make Him to be sin for us (2 Corinthians 5:21). He "learned obedience by the things which He suffered" (Hebrews 5:8).

Submission is obedience. Jesus was willing to submit to His Father in all things, even the most painful situations life could throw at Him. Understanding that, we must ask ourselves, "Am I willing to submit to legitimate authority?"

What does submission to authority include? Let's be specific and name a few:

* Submission to parents
* Submission to teachers
* Submission to God

* Submission to spiritual leaders
* Submission to the laws of the land
* Submission to husbands

Submit at Home

Obedience is first learned in the home with parents. Next it is learned at school with teachers, then at church with church leaders, and then in life as a citizen with civil authorities. When girls learn submission, they prevent enormous heartaches in the years ahead.

> Children, obey your parents in the Lord, for this is right. "Honor your father and mother" which is the first commandment with promise, "that it may be well with you and you may live long on the earth" (Ephesians 6:1–2).

A child's first authority figure is a biological parent or an alternate caretaker who assumes a parental role. If the child doesn't obey that first authority figure, she soon finds

Is It Wrong?

Think of one of your friends who is not submissive to her parents. Who is in transgression? Her or her parents?

Read the following perversions of scripture and answer the question following:

* *I will obey my parents when they are reasonable, sweet, and kind.*
* *I will obey God unless my close friends find my actions to fanatical.*

Why is it wrong to rationalize God's Word to suit my feelings?

My Obedience

I will work on being more obedient and submissive in these ways:

1. ______________________

____

____

____

2. ______________________

____

____

____

How does my obedience to parents and teachers relate to my obedience to God?

____

____

____

____

____

____

____

that life deals some hard blows. In fact, obedience to parents may very well protect the life of the child as a little one and as a teen. Let's face it, parents are more aware of the pitfalls of life—whether spiritual or physical—than children are. Obeying parents will bring a state of wellness to our lives, and we may enjoy a long life if we heed their warnings. That just makes sense.

Children who have learned the lessons of obedience at home adjust better to school rules and guidelines than children who have been allowed to have their own way.

I'm a schoolteacher. I've tested the validity of this statement a thousand times. There have been few exceptions. Submitting to parents is merely a prelude to submission to other authority figures such as teachers and policemen—and God.

As a child grows and gradually becomes conscious of good and evil, she has the ability to understand the gift of God's salvation—the age varies with each person. At that point of maturity, the understanding of her responsibility to submit to God in full obedience seems inherent. And in a sense it is. She has been trained from birth.

Obedience to God demands that we continue to obey our parents, and as we develop, we begin ever so gradually to submit to society's laws. When you reach the grand age of sixteen and receive the coveted driver's license, you must obey the civil authorities and laws of the land. Submission is obedience.

Chain of Command

Up to this point we've been able to see that obedience or submission is a universal reality. Regardless of gender and regardless of age, we all submit to someone or something. Teachers submit to principals, principals submit to superintendents, superintendents submit to boards, and boards submit to the communities and the

Is Obedience Kin to Love?

By this we know that we love the children of God, when we love God and keep His commandments. For this is the love of God, that we keep His commandments. And His commandments are not burdensome (1 John 5:2–3).

How do I show my love for God?

____

____

____

How can I obey His commands if I do not know them?

____

____

Why is knowing God's Word vital to obeying His will?

____

____

____

Male Leadership: God's Reasons

* Adam was made first (1 Tim. 2:13).
* Eve was made second (1 Tim. 2:13).
* Adam was not the one tricked by the devil (1 Tim. 2:14).
* Women should learn in quietness and full submission—he did not "permit a woman to teach or to have authority over a man" (1 Tim. 2:12).
* God designated men as elders and deacons to oversee and care for the work of the church (Acts 20:28; Heb. 13:17).

Female Leadership: God's Reasons

In the previous verses, the Bible teaches that women are not to have authority over men in spiritual matters, such as teaching, preaching, and visible

civil laws that direct them—all must ultimately submit to God or pay dire consequences. Obedience to rules or laws brings about safety and assurance within our homes and communities. If you desire an eternal reward, you must obey God.

Why is it so hard to understand and accept the roles of authority that God has placed in the church and in marriage? Scripture plainly teaches that from the beginning—before the fall of Adam and Eve—God established positions of authority, a chain of command in the physical home and in His spiritual family. Paul reminded Timothy that Adam was made first, and Eve was made later. He further said Adam was not the one tricked by the devil.

Choosing Your Husband, Being a Wife

When is a wife's submission to her husband not difficult; rather, a joy? When she has a husband who will die for her—when he loves her as himself. I'm glad we're looking at it from your side of marriage. You should be critically cautious in selecting a husband, because choosing a husband is one of the most important decisions you will make. Why? Because your husband will be the authority figure to whom you submit.

Also, your husband will be the father of your children and the authority figure to whom they will submit.

The Time Is Now!

At your age, marriage is probably not on your mind. But because the world has a totally different view of the role of women—and we all tend to adapt to our surroundings—the best time to learn the basic principles of obedience and submission is now. If you do not study and understand the truths about submission when you are young and pliable, you may be tempted to drift into the worldly pattern of female domination and leadership.

leadership roles in worship. Now find scriptures that command women to be public leaders in worship.

____

____

____

Future Wife

Wives, submit to your own husbands, as to the Lord. For the husband is the head of the wife as also Christ is the head of the church; and He is the Savior of the body. Therefore, just as the church is subject to Christ, so let the wives be to their own husbands in everything (Eph. 5:22–24).

Future Husband

Husbands, love your wives just as Christ also loved the church and gave Himself for her . . . So husbands ought to love their own wives as their own bodies; he who loves his wife loves himself (Eph. 5:25–28).

God's Girls vs. Culture

Counterculture
noun \ˈkau̇n-tər-ˌkəl-chər\

: a culture with values and morals that run counter to those of established society

What does it mean to be God's girl? Discuss in class the following accepted behavior in today's culture:

1. Male bashing
2. Girls always in the lead:
   ~Asking guys out
   ~Manipulating friendships
   ~Behaving sexually-suggestive
3. Girls in rebellion
4. Girls being mean on Facebook and cell phone texts (cowardly girls)

Knowing God's Word is essential to obeying His will. If your life is not anchored in truth, the lines between right and wrong will begin to blur as you grow older. Satan will lead you close to the edge of sin's cliff. How close can you get without falling over? Ignoring the rules is sometimes daring and alluring. And like that young photographer in Hawaii, when you get close enough to see the forbidden, the soft ground might give way and swallow you. Too late you discover that strong attractions camouflaged the real dangers. Too late you learn the real cost of disobedience.

No boundaries? No restrictions? No laws? Impossible! Such a society would fill our lives and surroundings with a sense of abandonment. Chaos would fill our communities with extreme dangers and no place of refuge. Our lives would be as a runaway train or a derelict ship. No hope.

Thankfully God has given us direction, a compass to help us navigate through life, warning signs to help us identify and avoid the pitfalls of sin. His Word is always available to guide our every thought and action. And it is quite possible that our obedience in the midst of a disobedient generation will have an eternal influence on others, leading them to the Lord and everlasting life.

For One Indulgent Moment

The cost for a moment's reckless folly is recorded several times in the Book of Ages. Check out the following list carefully and thoughtfully. Do you think for a moment these people got their "money's worth"?

1. Adam and Eve, for one bite of unknown fruit when they were not even hungry, brought sin, suffering, shame, and death upon themselves and the human race (Genesis 3).
2. Lot's wife, revealing her longing for the things that pertain to earth, took one look back at Sodom and became a pillar of salt (Genesis 19).
3. Esau, to satisfy one day's fleshly appetite, lightly esteemed his birthright and sold it for a morsel of food (Genesis 25).
4. Achan, for a garment he would never wear and for silver and gold he could not spend, paid with all his possessions, his family, and his life (Joshua 7).
5. Samson, for the cares of a hypocritical woman, lost his strength, his eyes, and finally his life (Judges 16).
6. David, to enjoy another man's wife, left a record of adultery, murder, shame, and tears boldly written for all to read (2 Samuel 11; Psalm 51).
7. Ahab, coveting another's little vineyard, permitted his wife to have its owner killed, claimed it for his own, and heard his own funeral preached in these words: "In the place where the dogs licked the blood of Naboth, dogs shall lick your blood, even yours" (1 Kings 21:19).

—Carroll Sites

In exchange for one indulgent moment, people surrender to the folly of sin. Could it be that many today are guilty of some of the same radical mistakes? Their rash decision may upset their whole life and the lives of others. It may condemn their souls and the souls of others. Think about it!

—Carroll Sites, Higden, Arkansas

Day	Bible Reading	Self-Check
1	Genesis 3	Today I will tell my father (or father-figure) of his importance in my life.
2	Philippians 2:8	Today I thank God for Jesus' great sacrifice.
3	Hebrews 5:8	Today I thank God for Jesus' obedient, submissive heart.
4	Psalm119:97	Today I thank God for His laws and commands.
5	1 Timothy 2:11–13; 3:1–7	Today I remember God's authority in His church.
6	Psalm 19:7–11	Today I commit my life to studying God's Word.
7	Ephesians 5:22–24	Today I commit my future to God. If one day I choose marriage, it will be to a faithful Christian man.

God's Girls Lead with Love

And now abide faith, hope, love, these three; but the greatest of these is love.

1 Corinthians 13:13

Christina already had the butter melting in the pan and the flour measured for the crust of her famous blueberry pie. Then—"Oops! no sugar!" She began a frantic search for a recipe for a sugarless pie. She flipped through the recipe book: apple pie, cherry pie, peach, banana, pineapple, chocolate—sugar, sugar, sugar, sugar! Christina came face to face with a cold, hard fact: *You just do not make a pie without sugar.*

What sugar is to pie, love is to Christian service. Service that honors Jesus Christ without love does not exist. No matter how you try to give loveless service to Jesus, your attempts will leave a bad taste in others' mouths.

Let's face it: the heart of leadership is the heart. Before we can properly use the tools of leadership, there must be a fundamental understanding of the vital role the heart plays in all we do. When we, as leaders, seek to guide others toward Jesus, we will often be in close company with the unlovable, unkind, impatient, and rude. Some of them will not only act contrary to God's will but will also attempt to wound us spiritually.

Donna Hates Me

Donna hates me because Gene asked me for a date last Friday. I know she hates me because she told me on Facebook she was going to mess up my pretty face. How can I possibly love her? I have a real problem. How can I do good to Donna, who is doing evil to me?

Love your enemies, bless those who curse you, do good to those who hate you, and pray for those who spitefully use you and persecute you (Matt. 5:44).

Your Enemies

The Jews had a rule of thumb: Love your neighbor but hate your enemy. Jesus spoke to them about their misunderstanding of God's command:

> But I say to you, love your enemies and pray for those who persecute you, so that you may be sons of your Father who is in heaven (Matthew 5:44 ESV).

He described the shallowness of love that did good only to those who did good to them. He reminded them that God gives good things, such as rain, to the evil and to the good. If we, then, are to be called children of God, we must be godly in our treatment of those who abuse or persecute us.

Don't Like Her Ways but Love Her

What did Jesus mean when He said, "Love your enemies"? Did He mean we have to enjoy their company—that we have to socialize with them? Did He mean we have to like them? If so, we have a difficult problem. But His expectations of us do not reach into those deep social relationships.

So what kind of love was Jesus talking about? He used a word that gives His command a very different meaning—*agape*. That special Greek word is very often used in Scripture to describe a committed love, one that transcends *phileo*—friendship love—and all other loves. Agape love is wholly devoted to the good of another. It will survive through all the likes and dislikes because it is committed.

Jesus did not command us to like our enemies. Aren't you glad of that? The enemy may be a person totally worldly, a person who treats us abusively at school or at work, a person who does not know God.

Love in Action

Refer to the previous text (Matt. 5:44) to complete the following blanks and see your enemy. At the same time, you will see in actions the love expected of you.

- Bless ______________________

- Do good ______________________

- Pray ______________________

For if you love those who love you, what reward have you? (Matt. 5:46).

Write a prayer for someone who is mistreating you.

____

____

____

____

____

agape
noun \ä-ˈgä-(ˌ)pā; ˈä-gə-ˌpā\
Unselfish love that considers the welfare of another; love that is ready to serve

In the past, when I was guilty of hating, cursing, using, or persecuting someone, what if that person prayed for me and treated me kindly? How would I have felt?

____

____

The Church of Great Price

Christ . . . loved the church and gave Himself for her (Eph. 5:25).

The church is important because of its purchase price, which was

____

This is the message you heard from the beginning, that we should love one another . . . By this we know love, because He laid down His life for us. And we also ought to lay down our lives for the brethren (1 John 3:11–16).

Sad to say, some of those individuals may even be our brothers and sisters in Christ who have briefly fallen into various sins of the heart. If this has not happened to you, be thankful, but stay on guard. You have a lifetime ahead, you are human, and Satan is powerful. Someone has well said, "Christians are not perfect; they're just saved." Yes, and we must concentrate on glorifying Christ in our salvation.

Christians Are the Church

When a brother or sister in Christ disappoints you so much you are about to throw him overboard, ask yourself: *Do I love Jesus?* Then ask: *Do I love the church?* It is easy to express love for Jesus but much harder to express love for those who comprise His body. But we cannot separate love for Jesus from our love for the church.

Our love for Christ cannot be compartmentalized in a tidy little box, while our dislike for the church is shelved in a not-so-tidy box. The church is the bride of Christ. How would a groom feel if someone treated him with love, yet mistreated his bride? The answer is simple; the groom would fiercely protect his bride. The same is true with the church of our Lord. Loving each individual Christian, even the ornery ones, is like loving Jesus.

And its opposite is true: showing disregard or hatred for those in the church is like showing disregard or hatred for Christ.

Thankfully, *agape* is the word used in 1 John 3:11–17. You don't have to like everyone, but in order to please Christ you must practice agape love. Make it a practice to return good for evil. You might win a soul for Christ.

Talk the Talk

Agape love might require that you go to an individual privately, speaking about her sinful attitude or action. "Oh, that's too difficult," you might say. "I just don't have that kind of attitude. My courage

She Hurt Me!

If your brother sins against you, go and tell him his fault between you and him alone (Matt. 18:15).

If I'm caught in a sin against you, I want you to keep it quiet. But if you offend me, I want to shout it to the world. Why is this kind of thinking wrong?

TIP: When feeling bitter toward a "friend" who has proved to be an enemy, try this: *Compare her mean actions to the worst sin you have ever committed.*

Motivated by Love

Though I speak with the tongues of men and of angels, but have not love, I have become sounding brass or a clanging cymbal. And though I have the gift of prophecy, and understand all mysteries and all knowledge, and though I have all faith, so that I could remove mountains, but have not love, I am nothing. And though I bestow all my goods to feed the poor, and though I give my body to be burned, but have not love, it profits me nothing (1 Cor. 13:1–3).

List every good work named in the above scripture. What must each have in order to be profitable?

____

____

____

____

____

____

would fail me." While you are thinking of yourself and the way you feel about it, would you like to think what Jesus said about that matter? Here is His analysis:

> If your brother sins against you, go and tell him his fault between you and him alone (Matthew 18:15).

Unfortunately, our first choice in resolving conflict does not usually take the commands of Jesus into consideration. We feel a need to gather as many friends as possible to side with us. Satan loves that position. He wants us to talk to everyone except the individual who has wronged us; he wants nothing but strife and division in the church. Jesus said we are even in danger of letting the strife hinder our worship (Matthew 5:23–24). We must go immediately to the person who has wronged us or to the person we have wronged. The longer we wait, the more our wound will fester. If we follow Jesus' plan and settle disagreements quickly and privately, then we exhibit an example of Jesus' leadership.

And one more thing: We should always remember to maintain a spirit of meekness (Galatians 6:1).

God's Girls Learn Love

Matters of the heart are vitally important as we search out our role as quiet leaders in the church. In fact, if we want God to acknowledge any good we try to accomplish as leaders, we must be motivated by pure love. Paul talked about this strong connection of leadership and love in 1 Corinthians 13.

Service is meaningless if love is not the motivating force. You may visit the elderly, care for a needy widow, give your clothes to the poor, or engage in any other worthy act of service. You may "give your body to be burned," but if you do not have agape love, the service becomes simply a rattling noise in God's ears.

If your motivation for service is simply to make

Show Your Christian Love

Love is patient and kind; love does not envy or boast; it is not arrogant or rude. It does not insist on its own way; it is not irritable or resentful; it does not rejoice at wrongdoing, but rejoices with the truth. Love bears all things, believes all things, hopes all things, endures all things (1 Cor. 13:4–5 ESV).

Use the previous scripture to complete the blanks below.

Do These Things:

____

____

____

____

Don't Do These Things:

____

____

____

____

yourself look good or to be seen by others or to have an impressive college entrance application, you have lost sight of the true spiritual meaning of leadership.

In 1 Corinthians 13:4–8 Paul described the kind of love God desires. Before we can properly use the tools of leadership, we must understand the role the heart plays in all we do. Scripture

Installing Love

Tech Support: Yes . . . how can I help you?

Customer: Well, after much consideration, I've decided to install Love. Can you guide me through the process?

Tech Support: Yes. I can. Are you ready to proceed?

Customer: Well, I'm not very technical, but I think I'm ready. What do I do first?

Tech Support: The first step is to open your Heart. Have you located your Heart?

Customer: Yes, but several other programs are running. Is it okay to install Love while they are running?

Tech Support: What programs are running?

Customer: Let's see, I have Past Hurt, Low Self-Esteem, Grudge, and Resentment running right now.

Tech Support: No problem. Love will gradually delete Past Hurt from your current operating system. It may remain in your permanent memory, but it will no longer disrupt other programs. Love will eventually override Low Self-Esteem with a module of its own called High Self-Esteem. However, you have to completely turn off Grudge and Resentment. Those programs prevent Love from being properly installed. Can you turn those off?

Customer: I don't know how. Can you tell me?

Tech Support: With pleasure. Go to your Start menu and delete Bitterness. Do this as many times as necessary until Grudge and Resentment are completely erased.

Customer: Okay, done. Love has started installing itself. Is that normal?

Tech Support: Yes, but remember that you have only the base program. You need to begin connecting to other Hearts in order to get the upgrades.

clearly shows that the heart of leadership is the heart of God's girl. "What sugar is to pie, love is to Christian service." Those in the world need to see that we have been seasoned with the sweetness of love so we can draw them to Christ. When agape love fills our souls and motivates us to serve, we will leave a good taste behind, and God will take notice.

Customer: Oops. I have an error message already. It says, "Error—Program not run on external components." What should I do?

Tech Support: Don't worry. It means that the Love program is set up to run on Internal Hearts, but has not yet been run on your Heart. In non-technical terms, it simply means you have to love yourself before you can love others.

Customer: So what should I do?

Tech Support: Pull down Self-Acceptance; then click on the following files: Forgive Self, Realize Your Worth, and Acknowledge Your Limitations.

Customer: Okay, done.

Tech Support: Now copy them to the "My Heart" directory. The system will overwrite any conflicting files and begin patching faulty programming. Also, you need to delete Verbose Self-Criticism from all directories and empty your Recycle Bin to make sure it is completely gone and never comes back.

Customer: Got it. Hey. My Heart is filling up with new files. Smile is playing on my monitor and Peace and Contentment are copying themselves all over my Heart. Is this normal?

Tech Support: Sometimes. For others, it takes a while. So Love is installed and running. One more thing before we hang up. Love is Freeware. Be sure to give it and its various components to everyone you meet. They will in turn share it with others and return some cool components back to you.

Customer: Thank you, God.

—Author Unknown

Leading in Daily Devotion

Day	Bible Reading	Self-Check—ask yourself . . .
1	Matthew 5:44	How do I express love to my enemies?
2	1 John 3:11	How do I express love to my physical family?
3	1 John 3:16	How do I know what love is?
4	Matthew 18:15	How do I respond when someone sins against me?
5	Matthew 5:23–24	How do I respond when I have hurt another person?
6	1 Corinthians 13:1–3	How does God regard my Christian service?
7	1 Corinthians 13:4–7	How do I express true love in my actions?

God's Girls Lead with Character and Decency

But also for this very reason, giving all diligence, add to your faith virtue, to virtue knowledge, to knowledge self-control, to self-control perseverance, to perseverance godliness, to godliness brotherly kindness, and to brotherly kindness love.

2 Peter 1:5–7

Young Abram cherished the sheet of paper his elderly friend gave him. Its intrinsic worth was zilch—nada. But its real worth? No appraiser would have touched it, because, you see, its value depended on the recipient. And you know the recipient, but we will talk about him later. For now, stick with the paper and its script, beginning with "Never be idle." Sound interesting? Keep reading.

Never be idle.
Make few promises.
Always speak the truth.
Live within your income.
Never speak evil of anyone.
Keep good company or none.
Live up to your engagements.
Never play games of chance.
Drink no intoxicating drinks.
Maintain good character above everything else.
Keep your own secrets if you have any.
Never borrow if you can possibly help it.
Wait till you are able to support a wife to marry.
Look into the eyes of the person to whom you are speaking.
Save when you are young and spend when you are old.
Never run into debt unless you can see a way out again.
Good company and good conversation are the sinews of virtue.
Your character cannot be essentially injured except by your own acts.
If anybody speaks evil of you, let your life be so that no one believes him.
When you retire at night think over what you have done during the day.
If your hands cannot be employed usefully, attend to the culture of your mind.
Read these rules carefully and thoughtfully at least once a week.

The young man kept the personal principles close to his heart until the end of his life. The simple guidelines are intriguing—they capture the essence of what it takes to develop a moral foundation that will sustain a person until old age.

Who was young Abram? James Abram Garfield, twentieth president of the United Sates and a baptized believer in Christ. You have the same opportunity as he did—read the rules at least once a week.

Watch!

As a young Christian woman, you have the ability to build good character, develop a sense of sound moral judgment, and build your faith. If you choose decency over indecency, morality above immorality, and Christianity instead of worldliness, you most likely will not attain fame and fortune. But as you grow spiritually, as you influence family members, as you work quietly in the church, and as you resist sinful influences of your peers and the media, rest assured, you will make a tremendously good impact on your home, on the church, and on the world.

Developing Moral Integrity

Today we call it building character or developing moral integrity. I wonder . . . when was the last time you heard the words *integrity, goodness, gratitude, honesty, self-control, sincerity,* or any word that describes moral strength of one's character. Those words

Building Destiny

Watch your thoughts, for they
become words.
Watch your words, for they
become actions.
Watch your actions for they
become habits.
Watch your habits for they
become your character.
Watch your character, for it
becomes your destiny.

—Source unknown

God Is Near

For indeed, those who are far from You shall perish . . . But it is good for me to draw near to God (Ps. 73:27–28).

Are God's promises real? Is God real? Can I practice knowing His presence? Is He near? Do I place God in a certain location, such as the church building, and then in every hour of the day never give Him a thought?

Here are my thoughts on these questions:

You heard my plea, "Do not close your ear to my cry for help!" You came near when I called on you; You said, "Do not fear!" (Lam. 3:56–57).

Seek the Lord . . . grope for Him and find Him, though He is not far from each one of us; for in Him we live and move and have our being (Acts 17:27–28).

Write three words that describe moral strength.

____

____

____

When I say several times a day, "God is near," how does that help me develop moral strength?

____

____

____

____

____

____

are not often heard in our modern society. And what a shame.

Young ladies have expressed to me a gross absence of gratitude or thankfulness among their peers, including their Christian friends. They report the scarcity of simple gestures such as kindness to a restaurant server, writing a brief thank-you note for a gift or special kindness, or saying a simple thank you. And equally alarming is the fact that cheating and lying have become the norm. Our society no longer promotes positive character traits but glorifies and rewards negative or undesirable characteristics. It is increasingly challenging for a young person to develop and maintain good character.

Thankfully for our sakes God has much to say about integrity and moral strength in both Old and New Testament—integrity (Psalm 78:72); courage (Acts 28:15); goodness (Galatians 5:22); gratitude (Colossians 3:15);

honesty (Hebrews 13:18); sincerity (2 Corinthians 1:12).

Building Blocks

When the apostle Peter wrote to those who had dedicated their lives to Jesus, he knew they would face intense persecution (2 Peter 1:5–8). The trials were severe and many would not escape the social, emotional, and physical struggles that Christians experienced in a first-century pagan society. They were asked to proclaim Caesar as Lord, Refusing to do so sometimes resulted in death. Christians were compelled to betray close friends, sisters, brothers, mothers, and fathers. Refusing to do so brought certain, immediate punishment, perhaps even death.

Peter knew that even though these early Christians proclaimed their faith in the risen Lord Jesus, they would have to build upon that faith in order to endure life's temptations. He told them to add to their faith

Esteem Others Better

Let each esteem others better than himself . . .look out not only for his own interests, but also for the interests of others (Phil. 2:3–4).

How do I consider others more important than myself?

____

____

____

____

____

Consider the comment, "Christians were compelled to betray close friends." How does this happen today?

____

____

____

____

____

____

My Virtues

Underline each of the following "building blocks" from 2 Peter 1:5–9 in the main text, including the previous page and these two pages.

Faith

Courage

Knowledge

Self-Control

Endurance

Godliness

Brotherly kindness

Love

As God's girl, I can build each of the above virtues. (Beside each word, write just one way to improve that particular trait.)

virtue—courage. When it wasn't popular to be a Christian, they needed toughness.

Then he told them to add knowledge to their courage. It was not enough to know and obey the first principles of salvation; they had to grow. It was not enough that they simply listen to good preaching. They had to test the preachers—make sure their words agreed with God's Word.

The Bereans did just that. They tested Paul's message and Luke, the inspired historian, complimented them, saying they were of more noble character because they examined the Scriptures daily (Acts 17:11).

Peter went on to encourage Christians to add to their knowledge, temperance—self-control. Once we identify sin as opposed to righteousness and choose to accept right living, we have practiced self-control. And each time we say no to sin, we draw ever closer to God.

Add to self-control, perseverance—endurance. Each time we conquer a temptation to sin, it is as if we have jumped another hurdle on our way to the finish line. The runner who has patient endurance is the one who will reach the finish line.

The apostle continued by saying: To perseverance we should add godliness—God-likeness. What does it mean to be Godlike? To find that answer, simply look to Jesus who was God come down to earth. When we question an action or thought, it is very appropriate to ask the sometimes trite question, "What would Jesus do?" If we are tempted to take a drug, to gossip about a classmate, or to use vulgar language, we should picture Jesus in that same situation and choose to be Christlike—Godlike—in all that we think, say, and do.

Finally, Peter instructed Christians to add to godliness, brotherly kindness, and to brotherly kindness, love. In fact, he said that one who

Giving all diligence, add to your faith virtue, to virtue knowledge, to knowledge self-control, to self-control perseverance, to perseverance godliness, to godliness brotherly kindness, and to brotherly kindness love. For if these things are yours and abound, you will be neither barren nor unfruitful in the knowledge of our Lord Jesus Christ (2 Pet. 1:5–8).

No Mind Wasting!

These were more noble than those in Thessalonica, in that they received the word with all readiness of mind, and searched the scriptures daily, whether those things were so (Acts 17:11 KJV).

What do I need to practice from the previous verse?

1. Receive the Word with

____

2. Search the

____

3. Search (How often?)

____

She said "No!" (Esther 1).

Imagine the horror . . . when the people got word that queen Vashti had flatly refused to do the bidding of their king. She took a great risk . . . yet Vashti had enough self-control and modesty to refuse him (Brenda Rollins, *Prescriptions for a Woman's Soul* [Huntsville, AL: Publishing Designs, Inc., 2008], pp. 58–59).

Queen Vashti was ordered to show her beauty before a group of drunken men. What did she do?

____

____

My Steps in Self-Control

1. Identify "sin."
2. Identify "doing right."
3. Choose "doing right."

In order to have self-control, I need to say ______ to sin.

does not have these qualities is nearsighted almost to blindness, forgetting that she has been cleansed from sin. On the contrary, if a Christian builds upon these foundation principles of good Christian character, she will bear much fruit for the kingdom of Christ.

Maintaining Spiritual Integrity

Satan has many cunning ways of drawing us away from God and weakening our spiritual integrity. Anything that keeps me from the study of God's Word or from being with Christians has the ability to draw my focus away from God and direct it to the world—including good activities. Is it possible for a young person to be so involved in good activities, such as clubs and civic duties, that she does not have time to get to know God? Yes. Let us never forget; Bible study and Christian fellowship are keys to developing decency and good character because they lead us to know more about God. They help us to grow spiritually.

Paul told Timothy to give attention to reading, to exhortation, and to doctrine. Do these traits show up in my daily routine? Paul understood the value of studying the doctrine of Christ and encouraging others to do so.

Love and Me

Jesus did not say, *Love God, only if you want to, and only when you want to.*

What did He say? *(Matt. 22:37)*

Consider the impact of the actions of each person within your Christian youth group. When on an excursion with the youth group, the world sees the name of the church on your T-shirts and on the side of the bus. When one of your group is disrespectful or rude, her conduct reflects on the entire group. Going against the flow requires courage and self-control, but we must stand for what is right. Don't hesitate to encourage others to be respectful and courteous and to treat strangers in the same kind way. The world is watching.

"Character Quotes"

The rule that governs my life is this: Anything that dims my vision of Christ, or takes away my taste for Bible study, or cramps my prayer life, or makes Christian work difficult, is wrong for me, and I must, as a Christian, turn away from it.

—Dr. J. Wilbur Chapman

Henry Wingblade used to say that Christian personality is hidden deep inside us. It is unseen, like the soup carried in a tureen high over a waiter's head. No one knows what's inside—unless the waiter is bumped. Just so, people don't know what's inside us until we've been bumped. But if Christ is living inside, what spills out is the fruit of the Spirit.

—Carl Lundquist

The best index to a person's character is how he treats people who can't do him any good, and how he treats people who can't fight back.

—Abigail Van Buren

Character is what you are in the dark.

—D. L. Moody

* Leading in Daily Devotion *

Day	Bible Reading	Self-Check
1	Psalm 78:72	Am I a person of integrity?
2	Acts 28:15	Am I a person of courage?
3	Colossians 3:15	Am I grateful?
4	Hebrews 13:18	Am I honest with myself and others?
5	Galatians 5:23	Am I practicing self-control?
6	2 Peter 1:5–8	Am I adding to my faith?
7	1 Timothy 4:12–13	Am I a good example to others?

CHAPTER 5

God's Girls Lead with a Good Attitude

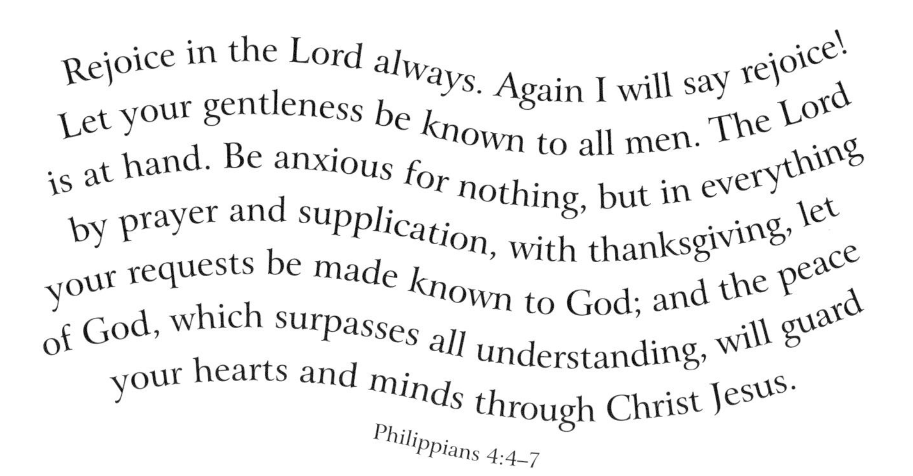

A city in the Netherlands had a great problem with litter. The sanitation department doubled the littering fine and increased the number of litter agents who patrolled the area. All efforts were to no avail. Then someone suggested that instead of punishing those who littered, they could reward people who properly disposed of garbage. Then some brainy fellow came up with the idea of a comedian trash can—one that told a joke when trash was deposited in it. The sanitation department bought it.

Different cans were programmed with different of jokes, and the recordings were changed every two weeks.

Guess what? Citizens went out of their way to keep their areas spruced up, and the streets were clean again. What made the difference? Positive leadership. People can be led to accomplish what seems impossible when they receive positive feedback for their efforts (Discipleship Journal, issue #48, p. 40).

reframe [ri-'freim] *verb (tr)*

To look at, present, or think of beliefs, ideas, relationships, etc. in a new or different way. *Example*: Reframe masculinity from this new perspective.

A Different Look

Imagine that you have a pair of large sunglasses with red lenses. Put them on. Does the world look different? As you put on these imaginary sunglasses, say to yourself, *Look through the eyes of Jesus!* Often if we look through the eyes of Jesus, we do not see the same hopeless situation as we saw even five minutes ago!

Reframing

Athletes and competitors have used the principle of positive reinforcement to achieve great things. Human nature is what it is—human nature. While the principle of accentuating the positive is used by many to succeed athletically, academically, and financially, it also applies spiritually when we are trying to lead others into paths of righteousness.

Through the years, I have observed that young ladies who become strong Christian leaders possess an enormous assurance in God. That assurance produces self-confidence. They possess an attitude of hopefulness. God gives them eternal hope, and this hope of heaven produces hope in all other areas of their lives. Their positive nature is simply contagious. They have the ability to reframe an event, a person, or a situation so they can remain positive in their focus and in their ability to lead others in a positive direction.

Are these individuals superhuman? No. In reality, many quickly admit they had to put aside some very negative characteristics—criticism, worrying, complaining, gossiping—before they could begin to succeed. Many lived within less-than-positive family settings. They had to learn to be positive in all things, a lesson that can be achieved at an early age. They learned to view life optimistically and to view people in a positive light. They learned how to see good even in adversity or the potential for good in the outcome.

Jesus' Model of Leadership

The characteristic of optimism is an essential ingredient of leadership. As we contemplate the positive nature of a good

Christ Can

Christ lives in me (Gal. 2:20).

I might say, "I can't"; "That won't work"; or "I'll never succeed." Have I forgotten? Christ lives in me! Am I saying "Christ can't"? How can I place myself under Christ's control and reframe problems through His eyes?

___

These things I have spoken to you, that in Me you may have peace. In the world you will have tribulation; but be of good cheer, I have overcome the world (John 16:33).

What is *tribulation*?

___

___

How do I know that I will—not might, but will—have tribulation?

___

Old Girl Buried

God's girl is a new girl; the old girl died and was buried in the baptism water. I must not let the old girl out of the grave! Did she worry, complain, and criticize? She might pop up to take over the new girl. I will put on my imaginary sunglasses, and say, "Christ lives in me!"

Why do so many Christian girls still have problems with their "old girl"?

____

How Things Look

Someone once said, "It's not how things look, it's how you look at things." How did Jesus put a different frame around the following?

Persecution ______________________________

Enemies ______________________________

Revenge ______________________________

THOUGHT: I am a Christian girl, not SuperGirl! I'm a human being, linked to Christ. If I were SuperGirl, would I need a Savior?

female leader, let us consider our leadership model, Jesus Christ. Throughout His ministry Jesus taught that one could and should reframe the events in our lives. Instead of feeling downcast when persecuted, you are to feel blessed and rejoice. That's what Jesus said (Matthew 5:10). If someone compels you to go one mile, go with him two (5:41). Instead of hating your enemy, love and bless him (5:44). Instead of seeking revenge, forgive. Just as surely as you do, your Father in heaven will forgive you (6:12).

These positive attitudes of the heart put a different frame, one of beauty, around what had been an ugly, negative event in our lives. The entire picture, the way we see ourselves and others, has been transformed. People want to be near us, to be near that kind of inner peace. This attitude of hopefulness acts as a magnet to draw people to you, just as men and women were drawn to this Man we call our Lord.

Jesus' Reaction to Complaints

As we reflect on Jesus' life, we don't see our Savior complaining, worrying, criticizing, or gossiping, even though He was often in the company of negative people—those who seemed to enjoy listening to their own complaints and criticisms of others. In fact, as we observe how many times Jesus confronted complaints and criticism, we should be in awe. You see, unlike any other human, He could read hearts. He knew the source of their complaints: jealousy, hatred, misunderstanding, and fear of the loss of power. He demonstrated extraordinary restraint as He gently responded to the whiners.

Jesus' Reaction to Criticism

Early in His ministry Jesus faced Jews who criticized Him because He said, "I am the bread which came down from heaven" (John 6:41). They reasoned that this man was

Get into Action!

Review the previous exercise answers: Rejoice! Love! Forgive! Jesus advised me to get into action instead of feeling downcast. Write some reframing action words beside these negatives:

Worry ______________________

Gossip ______________________

Whining ______________________

Jealousy ______________________

Criticism ______________________

By your words you will be justified, and by your words you will be condemned (Matt. 12:37).

If anyone desires to come after Me, let him deny himself, and take up his cross daily, and follow Me (Luke 9:23).

Jesus was a leader of action. Did He say, "I'll pull you along"? No! He said, "____________ ______."

Heart Reader

When Jesus reads my heart, what does He see? Cross out the negative traits.

that little boy, grown up now, they had known as the son of Joseph and Mary, so how could He go around telling folks He came down from heaven? Jesus reminded them of their ancestors who ate manna in the wilderness and died. He said,

> I am the living bread which came down from heaven. If anyone eats of this bread, he will live forever; and the bread that I shall give is My flesh, which I shall give for the life of the world (John 6:51).

Despite His words of hope, they continued to quarrel, refusing to open their hearts and minds to the one who offered them eternal life. John goes on to tell us that even some of His disciples did not understand when they heard His teaching concerning eating His flesh and drinking His blood. They complained about this teaching, and from that time "many of His disciples went back and walked with Him no more" (John 6:66).

Focusing on Good

Jesus was at the home of Zacchaeus, a place no decent man would ever go—or so they thought (Luke 5:30; 15:2). The Pharisees and scribes identified Zacchaeus and his kind as the worst of sinners—Jewish tax collectors working for the Romans—traitors, without a doubt. *And He claims to be the Son of God.* Those of that strict Jewish sect were irate. Jesus seemed oblivious to their complaints and calmly assured those gathered there:

> Today salvation has come to this house, because he also is a son of Abraham; for the Son of Man has come to seek and to save that which was lost (Luke 19:9–10).

Jesus saw the good in Zacchaeus, instead of focusing on his flaws.

Jesus, our model of leadership, saw the potential for good in others, even in the

The Eyes of Jesus

When Jesus looked at the following individuals, what did He see? (Look in the main text on the next page.)

1. Matthew, the tax collector

____

____

2. James, the fisherman

____

____

3. Woman, a prostitute

____

____

4. Thomas, the doubter

____

____

5. Saul, the murderer

____

____

It's a Command

Read the following verses and underline the words that represent these major worry sources:

1. Getting old
2. Clothes
3. Food

And who of you by being worried can add a single hour to his life? And why are you worried about clothing? Observe how the lilies of the field grow; they do not toil nor do they spin, yet I say to you that not even Solomon in all his glory clothed himself like one of these. But if God so clothes the grass of the field, which is alive today and tomorrow is thrown into the furnace, will He not much more clothe you? You of little faith! Do not worry then, saying, "What will we eat?" or "What will we drink?" or "What will we wear for clothing?" (Matt. 6:27–31 NASB).

Complete this sentence from the above text:

_____ ________ *worry.*

most sinful. A tax collector could become a Gospel writer (Matthew), a fisherman could be transformed into a preacher (James), a prostitute could anoint a King, a doubter could see and believe (Thomas), a loose-tongued apostle could introduce the Gentiles to a risen Lord (Peter in the house of Cornelius), and a murderer (Saul of Tarsus) could travel the world telling the old, old story.

Setting Aside Worry

In His Sermon on the Mount, Jesus pointed believers toward a positive outlook in life—a different way of thinking (Matthew 6:27–30). A young person can fall into the pit of worry just as easily as an older person can. In fact, on many levels, anxiety is familiar to the young.

Does worry pull you into its grip? Do you feel the need to pop some pill to calm you down at the thought of a test or a speech or meeting a certain guy in the hall? Is your hair too curly or too straight? Are you worried that the car will break down or you'll have an accident? Some of the "action" suggestions might be of help to you.

The apostle Paul categorized worry as a sin in Philippians 4:6. Then he gave the antidote: prayer and thanksgiving. How's that for action? He follows by telling us what to keep in our minds—and worry is not on the list. (Read it for yourself: Philippians 4:8.)

Worrying is a waste of time and energy.

Think on Good Things

Paul advised believers to guard their thinking—to meditate on things that are true, noble, just, lovely, and of good report, with the promise again that the person who keeps this "mind of Christ" will have the peace of God. This type of leader influences others for good. Solomon taught the importance of meditating on good things when he said, "For

My Heart Guard—Peace!

Be anxious for nothing, but in everything by prayer and supplication, with thanksgiving, let your requests be made known to God; and the peace of God, which surpasses all understanding, will guard your hearts and minds through Christ Jesus (Phil. 4:6–7).

The peace of God is active. What will it do?

____

Why does my heart need a guard?

____

Too Much to Do!

How am I using my time? (Fill in approximate time each day invested in the following):

___ School
___ Texting friends
___ Bible study
___ Meals
___ Facebook
___ Homework
___ Christian friends
___ Prayer
___ Sleep

What areas above need more of my time? Circle them. Then cross out the areas that need less time.

Therefore let us pursue the things which make for peace and the things by which one may edify another (Rom. 14:19).

What can I do today to "edify another"?

____

____

____

____

____

____

as he thinks in his heart, so is he" (Proverbs 23:7).

As a young woman desiring to lead others, ask yourself these questions:

1. Do I worry a lot?
2. Am I constantly focused on the misdeeds of others?
3. Am I critical of others?
4. Am I a whiner, a complainer, a grumbler?

If the answer to any of these is yes, make a commitment to mend your ways. Worries, complaints, and criticism serve only to hinder the work of the Lord.

Back to the problem of trash in the Netherlands. The leaders found out that people motivated by positive words and rewards can soar in accomplishment! God's eternal reward is awaiting all the faithful in Christ. Your positive thoughts and actions help you reach heaven and take others with you. Decide today that you will lead with a good attitude.

"Attitude Quotes"

Happiness is a perfume you cannot pour on others without getting a few drops on yourself.

—Ralph Waldo Emerson

The winner glories in the good; the whiner majors in the mediocre. A winner's thinking process differs from that of others. As part of their normal moment-to-moment stream of consciousness, winners think constantly in terms of I can and I will. Losers concentrate their waking thoughts on what they should have done, would have done, and can't do. When the mind's self-talk is positive, performance is more likely to be successful. The huge majority of our negative doubts and fears are imaginary or beyond our control.

—Denis Waitley

A kicking mule doesn't pull, and a pulling mule doesn't kick.

—Unknown

Day	Bible Reading	Self-Check
1	Matthew 5:41	Today I will go the second mile even for my enemy.
2	Matthew 5:44	Today I will return good for evil.
3	James 4:11	Today I will set aside criticism and I will praise others.
4	Luke 19:9–10	Today I will be hopeful because of my hope in Christ.
5	Matthew 7:1–6	Today I will look inward instead of outward.
6	Philippians 4:4–7	Today I will set aside worry and trust God in prayer.
7	Proverbs 23:7	Today I will meditate on good things.

God's Girls Lead with Contentment

I have learned in whatever situation I am to be content. I know how to be brought low, and I know how to abound. In any and every circumstance, I have learned the secret of facing plenty and hunger, abundance and need. I can do all things through him who strengthens me.

Philippians 4:11–13 (ESV)

Russell Conwell, a nineteenth century orator, became famous for his "Acres of Diamonds," a true story he told more than six thousand times. By presenting the story, he raised enough money to establish Temple University in Philadelphia. Here is the gist of Conwell's story.

> Ali Hafed lived near the River Indus in ancient Persia. A sage from the East came by his farm one day and told him how the earth was made. "Diamonds were made last," he explained. "They are congealed drops of

sunlight, so they are the most expensive of all jewels." The sage went on to say that a diamond the size of a man's thumb could purchase the entire country.

Ali sold his farm, pocketed the money, and wandered far and near in search of diamonds. His quest led him into Palestine and then into Europe. He searched diligently throughout the continent. By the time he reached Barcelona, Spain, he was a poor, afflicted, suffering man. As he began to watch the waves rolling in between the Pillars of Hercules, he was overcome by the temptation to throw himself into the raging tide. His lifeless body sank beneath its foaming crest.

Do you suppose we're somewhat like poor Ali Hafed? Do we search and search for a "diamond" in our lives, that special something that would finally bring us contentment and a sense of fulfillment without ever considering what we already have?

I Have Enough

Self-control holds hands with contentment. Make it your motto to say, "I have enough" (Brenda Rollins, *Prescriptions for a Woman's Soul* [Huntsville, AL: Publishing Designs, Inc., 2008], p. 52).

After each of the following statements, write "I have enough" on the blank line.

I want a new car.

____

Sarah's haircut is cuter than mine.

____

Wish and Want

Contentment is a state of satisfaction. Its counterpart, discontentment, is a state of restlessness or dissatisfaction. Talk to women, young or old, and you'll hear, "If only I could have . . ." or, "I wish I was . . ." The wish list may include attributes or traits of character such as: "I wish I was confident, more outgoing." Or the list may have more tangible things: "I wish I could be beautiful, model a ritzy wardrobe, and drive around in a new Ferrari," Or the wish may be even simpler: "Why can't I be thin?" Does all that sound familiar?

Young Christians may not realize that wishes and wants have the ability to grow into more serious, sinful attitudes of the heart. Desire can morph into greed if it moves unchecked. When a friend has a new sweater or shoes you've been dying for, jealousy may be at the door. The attitudes of jealousy or covetousness can continue to spiral downward into the sin of envy, when you are eaten up with desire to have what belongs to another. Watch out for these sins when you begin thinking you would resort to anything, even something sinful—gossip, lies, thievery—to get what you want.

God's Word speaks about these sins that are born of discontent.

1. Achan's unbridled lust for the great spoils of Jericho caused him to take that which had been dedicated to God. His selfish act

I want another pizza.

____

If only Aldan would go with me.

____

Why can't I be skinny like Rosa?

____

Find two scriptures on contentment and write the references here:

1. ______________________________

2. ______________________________

The Beast of "More!"

Having food and clothing, with these we shall be content (1 Tim. 6:8).

What have I enjoyed today that is more than food and clothing? Controlled temperature in a house? Light at the touch of a button? Hot water? List at least four more "luxuries":

1. ______________________________

2. ______________________________

3. ______________________________

4. ______________________________

Treasure "If"

Go, sell what you have and give to the poor, and you will have treasure in heaven; and come, follow Me (Matt. 19:21).

What prompted, Jesus command in the previous verse?

___

___

___

Jesus did not say, "I like you! I'm going to reward you with treasure!" How was the "treasure in heaven" a conditional reward?

___

___

___

Underline all the action verbs in Matthew 19:21 above, and then write them here:

___

___

___

caused the deaths of thirty-six innocent men at the town of Ai, which in turn brought a stoning death to him and his entire family (Joshua 7:2–25).

2. Balaam's greed caused him to lose favor with God (Jude 11).
3. Our envy and covetousness, spurs of discontent, are right alongside the sins of wickedness, sexual immorality, maliciousness, murder, strife, deceit, and evil-mindedness in Romans 1:20–32.

God's Remedy for Discontentment

The Bible clearly shows that we should be content with the material things that surround us. Paul told Timothy,

> Now godliness with contentment is great gain. For we brought nothing into this world, and it is certain we can carry nothing out. And having food and clothing, with

these we shall be content (1 Timothy 6:6–8).

He continued by warning Timothy of the dangers of allowing a lack of material things to bring discontentment. Paul said those who desire to be rich fall into a snare, "for the love of money is a root of all kinds of evil" (1 Timothy 6:10).

Discontentment is a beast we all face. And as Christian women with the Lord on our side, we strive to conquer that beast. His Word allows us to see the bitter consequences of discontentment. If the desires of our heart center on beauty, popularity, fame, and fortune, we will fall into many temptations.

Dissatisfaction as a Motivation

While God's Word lets us know that discontentment should not be part of the Christian life, the Bible reveals that dissatisfaction in some areas can be a good thing, a motivation of sorts. In fact,

Carry Nothing Out

Imagine that the richest person you know has just died. How much wealth was left behind?

Circle your answer:

All of it

Some of it

None of it

Find a lesson given by Jesus in the New Testament about a rich man and a poor beggar. Write the reference here, and write the lesson in your own words.

My Spiritual Wish List

Is it easy to make a shopping list, or a wish list for a "makeover" at the spa? Why not keep a list of spiritual priorities? Include specific ways of seeking His righteousness and His Kingdom (the church).

1. ____________________

2. ____________________

3. ____________________

4. ____________________

I Shall Not Lack

Oh, taste and see that the Lord is good; blessed is the man who trusts in Him! Oh, fear the Lord, you His saints! There is no want to those who fear Him . . . those who seek the Lord shall not lack any good thing (Ps. 34:8–10).

Put your name in the blanks below:

Oh, fear the Lord, ___________! There is no want to ___________ who fears Him . . . ___________ who seeks the Lord shall not lack any good thing.

Jesus said there are certain things we should seek—we should long for them, earnestly desire them. What are those things?

Our Savior wants us to desire spiritual things so much that they take priority over the physical matters of life. In fact, He said if we let this priority rule our lives, God will give us all the material things we need. Jesus said,

> Seek first the kingdom of God and His righteousness, and all these things shall be added to you (Matthew 6:33).

We should desire those things that help us reach heaven (Psalm 34:8–10).

Spiritual Perfection in Jesus

The apostle Paul learned to be content, whether living in luxury or living as a shackled prisoner in a dark dungeon. He experienced both. Whether he was in the midst of plenty or in the clutches of poverty, he was content because his focus was on Jesus and eternal life. In other words, Paul sought spiritual completeness that is found only in Christ Jesus through faith, trust, and obedience.

He refused to be centered on the world and its trappings. Rather, he claimed citizenship in an eternal kingdom. Because of his intense desire to be eternally in the Lord's presence, he sought every opportunity to improve the condition of his soul and the souls of others.

What State Is That?

When I sing, "This world is not my home / I'm just'a passing through," I am singing of the perfect "state of contentment"—heaven!

Our citizenship is in __________, from which we also eagerly wait for the Savior, the Lord Jesus Christ, who will transform our lowly body that it may be conformed to His glorious body (Phil. 3:20–21).

Do you remember Ali Hafed and his desire to possess diamonds? Ali never achieved that lofty goal. His disappointment and discontent led him to commit suicide. Now, here's the rest of the story.

> One day the man who purchased Ali Hafed's farm led his camel into the garden to drink. As the camel put its nose into the brook, the man saw a flash of light from the sands at the bottom of the stream. A pretty rock it was, reflecting all the hues of a rainbow, so he waded in, retrieved it, took it home, and laid it on his mantel.
>
> Not many days after, the sage who had visited Ali returned to his old farm. As the new owner admitted him, a flash of light from the mantel caught sage's eye. He rushed up to it, took one look, and shouted, "Here is a diamond. Has Ali returned?"

"Oh no. Ali Hafed has not returned, and that is not a diamond. That is nothing but a beautiful stone I found right out here in my garden stream."

"But I tell you," the sage asserted, "I know a diamond when I see one. I know positively this is a diamond."

The two walked out into the garden. The sage reached down and stirred the "rocky" soil. Diamonds. Those rocks were diamonds. Big ones, small ones—some far more beautiful than the one on the mantel.

The man had discovered the diamond mine of Golcanda, the most magnificent mine in all history. Kohinoor, the crown jewel of England, and Orloff, the crown jewel of Russia, came from that mine. Had Ali Hafed remained at home and dug in his own garden, instead of choosing death in a strange land, he would have had acres of diamonds.

Perhaps we must ask, "Do we sometimes act like Ali Hafed?" After all, we could search the world over for that special something that would finally bring us contentment and a sense of fulfillment, while the "diamonds" we are seeking are already in our possession. Jesus creates within us the peace of salvation and the hope of heaven. What a Rock!

We just need to stay home and dig a bit in the garden of our own heart. Let us allow God's Word to help us focus on Jesus, focus on spiritual things until we reach perfection or completeness. And until we see our Lord face to face, let us approach life with contentment and a sense of fulfillment, for God has truly filled us with everything we need for life and godliness.

Leading in Daily Devotion

Day	Bible Reading	Self-Check
1	Jude 11	Am I tempted by the sin of greed?
2	Joshua 7	Am I enticed to own things of which God would disapprove?
3	Romans 1:20–32	Am I conscious of the serious nature of envy?
4	1 Timothy 6:6–8	Am I contented?
5	1 Timothy 6:9	Am I tempted by the desire to be rich?
6	Matthew 6:33	Am I seeking first the kingdom of God and His righteousness?
7	Psalm 34:8–10	Am I focused on God's blessings?

God's Girls Lead with Humility

Therefore humble yourselves under the mighty hand of God, that He may exalt you in due time.

1 Peter 5:6

Two mountain goats meet on a narrow ledge. On the left is a sheer cliff, and on the right, a steep wall. The path is wide enough for only one animal to pass. The two are facing each other, and it is impossible for either to turn or back up. What a dilemma!

If the goats were people, they would probably start butting each other until at least one of them plunged into the chasm. But the goats know instinctively how to solve the problem. One of them lies down on the trail and the other goat walks over him. Then both are safe.

Humility. The goat's lying down is an accurate demonstration of what humble means: "low, not proud or haughty, not arrogant." One who is humble is willing to be lowly—on the ground, so to speak.

Let Somebody Else Do It

"Do not draw near this place. Take your sandals off your feet, for the place where you stand is holy ground" . . . And Moses hid his face, for he was afraid to look upon God . . . "I will send you to Pharaoh that you may bring My people, the children of Israel, out of Egypt." But Moses said to God, "Who am I that I should go to Pharaoh, and that I should bring the children of Israel out of Egypt?" (Exod. 3:5–6; 10–11).

How do we sometimes conclude that someone is humble, when the truth is they are afraid?

____

____

____

Why do you think Moses was afraid?

____

____

____

Take Your Sandals Off

One day when Moses was on the back side of the desert watching his sheep, a bush ignited, seemingly on its own, and began to burn without being consumed. Curious, Moses drew closer. Then something extraordinary happened.

"Moses, Moses!" It was the voice of God.

Moses was frightened. "Here I am."

"Do not draw near this place. Take your sandals off your feet, for the place where you stand is holy ground."

Moses hid his face. God continued to speak, telling him that He had heard the cries of His people. Moses was to go to Pharaoh, get them released, and bring them into a new land.

Moses was convinced he was not qualified for the job, so he began immediately to reject God's proposal with feeble excuses—four of them altogether. His last excuse told the whole story: "O my Lord, please send by the hand of whomever else You may send." In other words, "I don't want to go."

Moses saw himself as a very lowly being, but actually he was filled with pride. He thought he could outtalk God, but the Lord didn't let him excuse his way out of the job. And the result was great. Moses confronted Pharaoh face to face, stood up under the ridicule of the Israelites, and led God's people triumphantly out of Egyptian slavery.

A Family Fuss

In the wilderness, the people became restless and disobedient. Moses' own sister, Miriam—you know, the girl who watched over his little basket as it floated in the Nile among the bulrushes—turned against him. She and their brother Aaron spoke against Moses. The two of them didn't like the Ethiopian wife Moses had taken, and they believed their leadership of the Hebrews was just as important as

Write God's words to Moses from Exodus 3:12:

"*I will* ________________ ____

________ _______."

How do these words from God give me comfort today?

____

____

____

____

____

____

____

____

____

____

Write your name in the following blank, and read the verse aloud.

God has not given ___________
a spirit of fear, but of power and of love and of a sound mind
(2 Tim. 1:7).

God's Vengeance

Define *vengeance*.

How did Moses react to the hostility of his sister and brother?

Why do I sometimes want to "fix" the people who are mean to me?

Who took vengeance on Aaron and Miriam?

How can I allow God to handle situations beyond my control?

Look up Romans 12:19 and write the verse below:

Moses' leadership. Even in the face of such hostile attitudes and words, Moses didn't rush to his own defense. He waited for God to handle the situation, because Moses "was very humble, more than all men who were on the face of the earth" (Numbers 12:3). He had come a long way since his prideful and scary day at the Mount Sinai's burning bush. God humbled Miriam and Aaron, even to the extent of afflicting Miriam with leprosy.

Aaron and Miriam hung their heads in penitent shame. Moses kept a calm, meek attitude. He recognized the greatness of God, and his own insignificance in God's presence. Moses discovered and embraced true humility.

Another Humble Leader

After Moses' death, Joshua became the leader of God's people. When he crossed the Jordan on dry land, the hearts of the Canaanites who lived by the sea melted, "and there was no spirit in them any longer because of the children of Israel" (Joshua 5:1).

As Joshua was preparing to conquer Jericho, he was confronted by a Man who identified himself as the Commander of the army of the Lord. Joshua fell on his face and worshiped.

"Take your sandal off your foot," the Commander told him, "for the place where you stand is holy." Joshua was a humble man. He recognized the greatness of God and his own unworthiness (Joshua 5:13–15).

Joshua followed the Commander's instructions completely—the daily marches, the blast of the rams' horns, and the shout. God blessed him with a great victory over Jericho. The walls came tumbling down. Thank you, Joshua. Yours is the spirit of humility.

Women on Welfare

Elimelech and Naomi and their two sons, Mahlon and Chilion, left Bethlehem because of a

Holy Ground

And Joshua fell on his face to the earth and worshiped, and said to Him, "What does my Lord say to His servant?" (Josh. 5:14).

Research: When people of the Bible came into God's presence, what posture did they take? Give at least two examples, other than Joshua.

How would my life change, if every morning upon awakening I asked, "What does my Lord say to me, His servant?"

Where You Go, I'll Go

Ruth said to Naomi: "All that you say to me I will do" (Ruth 3:5).

In spite of her widowed state, her poverty, and her absence from her homeland, what was Ruth's general outlook on life?

____

____

____

Your daughter-in-law, who loves you . . . is better to you than seven sons (Ruth 4:15).

Many of God's girls will be daughters-in-law. Why should today's daughters-in-law hold up Ruth as a good example?

____

____

____

____

____

____

famine and moved to Moab. One of the sons took Ruth as his wife, and the other took Orpah, both Moabite women. The book of Ruth opens with these sketchy details and moves quickly to the death of Elimelech. Soon after, both Mahlon and Chilion died, leaving the three women alone. Grief stricken, Naomi decided to return to Bethlehem. She encouraged her daughters-in-law to remain in Moab, remarry, and have children. Ruth chose rather to go with her mother-in-law (Ruth 1:16–17).

In Bethlehem she and Naomi faced an obvious problem—supporting themselves. Thankfully, God had developed a welfare system for the poor. His law required farmers to leave a certain amount of grain in a field for those who had no land and could not otherwise provide for themselves. So Ruth went to gather grain for her and Naomi.

"And she happened to come to the part of the field belonging to Boaz, a man of the family of Elimelech"

(Ruth 2:3). Ruth had no idea how Naomi's God Jehovah was working in her life. She was a foreigner engaging in a very humbling experience. She was probably frightened, fearing for the welfare of her mother-in-law and of being in a strange country, among strange people, in a strange field. But she committed without reservation to this strangeness, including the acceptance of Naomi's God, Jehovah.

Boaz commended her for her loyalty to Naomi. He asked her to work in his field with the women he had employed. She was to drink of the water his men had drawn, not from "welfare" water she had brought. And further, he assured her that he had commanded the men not to touch her.

At His Feet

When she returned home that evening, Naomi informed Ruth of her eligibility to be Boaz's wife, for he was a kinsman of Elimelech. Then Naomi began to coach her in the cultural

A Loyal Proselyte

Look up the word *proselyte*. Write the definition below, and explain how this word describes Ruth.

____

____

____

____

____

____

____

____

____

____

Boaz recognized Ruth's loyalty to her mother-in-law. Write three specific ways that Ruth was loyal to Naomi.

1. ____________________

2. ____________________

3. ____________________

Jesus' Humility and Obedience

And being found in appearance as a man . . . (Phil. 2:8).

Jesus took on the form of a human being—and not a really handsome one, at that (Isa. 53:2). His human form housed His Spirit—God! How was this humbling for Jesus?

____

____

____

____

____

____

He humbled Himself and became obedient to the point of . . . death on the cross (Phil. 2:8).

Which comes first: humility or obedience?

____

"do's" and "don'ts" of a young single woman in Bethlehem. When Naomi asked Ruth go to the threshing floor where Boaz was winnowing barley and lie at his feet when he went to sleep, Ruth obediently took that lowly position. Boaz soon took Ruth as his wife. Ruth's son, Obed, was the grandfather of King David. Ruth's loyalty to Naomi and her humble obedience to Naomi's instruction put her in the lineage of Christ (Matthew 1:5). In the company of the humble we find Ruth.

He Humbled Himself

The Bible records examples of many others who were humble, but there is one more we must not overlook. From the viewpoint of those in His Galilean city, He had a pretty shaky beginning. He was conceived by a young woman, not quite single and not quite married. He was born in a stable; His first bed was a feeding trough for animals. His social status wasn't grand.

He was the son of a carpenter in Nazareth. He had no allowance. And as a young adult, His financial portfolio was nonexistent. He had nowhere to lay His head. And finally, He suffered the death of a criminal, all the while being absolutely free from sin. This man was the Son of God. The greatest example of humility was Jesus Christ.

How could someone of such knowledge, power, and glory become an ordinary man of flesh and blood? How could He live such a lowly life knowing He was due the praise and honor of creation? The answer is humility. Paul explained it this way:

> And being found in appearance as a man, He humbled Himself and became obedient to the point of death, even the death of the cross. Therefore, God also has highly exalted Him and given Him the name which is above every name (Philippians 2:8–9).

My Humility and Obedience

Let this mind be in you which was also in Christ Jesus (Phil. 2:5).

Is Philippians 2:5 a suggestion or a command?

____

"This mind which was also in Jesus"—what does this mean to me?

____

____

____

____

How can I humble myself to God's will?

____

____

____

____

Jesus met sin and sinful man on a mountain path with a sheer cliff on the left and a steep wall on the right. How could He save man? He did what any savior would do. He lowered Himself; He went to the ground and allowed sin and sinful man to walk over Him. The result? Breathtaking. God highly exalted Him and gave Him a name above all other names. What happened to sinful man? Man was saved because Jesus took that lowly position. He let us walk on Him.

Moses, Joshua, Ruth, and Jesus are in the company of the humble. Do we want to be named with the humble? If we are constantly butting heads, trying to have our own way and giving pride the upper hand, the result could be disastrous. Instead, let's practice humility in the home with our families, in the church with our church family, in the school with our classmates, and in the community and in the workplace with our neighbors. Let us have the sense of a billy goat. Better yet, let us have the humble nature of Jesus.

Leading in Daily Devotion

Day	Bible Reading	Self-Check
1	Luke 1:30–39	Do I respond with humble obedience to God's commands?
2	Numbers 12:3	On a scale of one to ten, how would those who really know me score my humility? God gave Moses a ten!
3	Joshua 5:13–15	Do I realize Jesus, the Commander, is always by my side?
4	Ruth 1:16	Do I obey my parents, teachers, and other people of authority?
5	Matthew 1:5	Is my name written in the Book of Life?
6	Philippians 2:8–9	What am I willing to sacrifice for Jesus?
7	Philippians 2:10–11	Am I willing to confess that Jesus Christ is Lord?

God's Girls Lead with Appearance

Women should adorn themselves in respectable apparel, with modesty and self-control . . . with what is proper for women who profess godliness—with good works.

1 Timothy 2:9–10 (ESV)

It's 6:30 Monday morning, and this week has to start right. Josie's in a frenzie because of last Friday night's great event. That cute Mason threw the winning touchdown pass in the big game. Half the girls in Josie's homeroom already had a crush on him; now it will be all the girls!

Oh, Mason must notice me today! He is, like, soooo cool. If I can just catch his eye, I know he will like me. And I have, like, the perfect chance, because he sits right behind me in geometry.

Oh, what to wear? Well . . . I haven't worn this skirt and sweater in a while because it's—well, I thought last time I wore it, maybe the skirt's, like, a little short, but it's, like, just right for today! And this almost-off-the-shoulder sweater is so cute and the blue, and it, like, makes my eyes sparkle. Mom picked out another sweater, but, well, you know Mom—it's a granny sweater.

Time's up! I'm wearing this skirt and sweater. Mom's in the kitchen so I'll just yell good-bye and scoot out the front door. I'll be extra careful to, like, adjust my sweater if I have to reach for anything, and I'll, like, keep a book on my lap when I am at my desk. This cool outfit should get this week started right!

Let's face it. Young women are bombarded from every side with questions and comments about their clothing. Magazines lead them to believe beauty must be packaged in a certain way. The music videos on television cast unclothed young women as fashionable, hip-hop, and most of all, desirable to the opposite sex. Peer pressure urges today's young ladies to push the envelope with parent and school dress codes. Parental restrictions on a young woman's clothing are often the source of harsh words and sour attitudes on everyone's part. Decisions about clothing are among the first life-decisions a girl makes.

If you wonder how something as simple as a decision about what to wear could set a tone for your entire life, take a brief look at Bathsheba (2 Samuel 11:1–17). She was in the wrong place, at the wrong time, wearing the wrong thing. The result was an adulterous affair, an unwanted pregnancy, the murder of her husband, and the death of her baby. Each tragedy might have been avoided if she had been wearing modest, proper clothing when David gawked at her from his rooftop.

The Difference Makes a Difference

So what's a girl to do? What's a *Christian* girl to do?

First, understand males and females, particularly their respective and unique responses to the opposite sex. The differences begin early on. Put simply, males and females are wired differently.

In studies of babies in hospital nurseries during the first three days of their little lives, the most common observation about baby girls was the movement of their mouths. The most common observation about the baby boys was the abundant movement of their hands, arms, legs, and feet. Believe it or not, those characteristics continue to blossom and become more pronounced with each passing year. God designed males and females in remarkably different ways.

Emotion in Motion

What are girls' unique characteristics? We love to

Check the Wiring

Are boys better than girls? Are girls better than boys? Discuss how God made us different—not one better than the other.

There is neither male nor female: for ye are all one in Christ Jesus (Gal. 3:28).

Read Galatians 3:28 from your Bible. What other contrasting groups fall into the category of "one in Christ Jesus"?

Girls and Guys

List 2 characteristics common in girls:

1. ____________________________

2. ____________________________

List 2 characteristics common in guys:

1. ____________________________

2. ____________________________

Ogle verb \'ō-gəl *also* 'ä-\
: to glance with amorous invitation or challenge
: to eye amorously or provocatively
: to look at especially with greedy or interested attention
Example: He sat at the bar, ogling several women.

I made a solemn pact with myself never to undress a girl with my eyes. So what can I expect from God? What do I deserve from God Almighty above? Isn't calamity reserved for the wicked? Isn't disaster supposed to strike those who do wrong? Isn't God looking, observing how I live? Doesn't he mark every step I take? (Job 31:1–4 MSG).

talk, so the friendship or relationship we cherish most is one in which we can talk about anything and be understood. We are emotion driven. Emotions guide us in almost every aspect of life, even in decision-making. Females are natural born nurturers. Caring for others' needs is an inborn trait, noticeable in our relationship with our first baby doll. Summed up, we want to be listened to, cared for, and, most of all, loved. When our emotional needs are met, we're agreeable, nurturing, and somewhat vulnerable. We talk often about love and marriage, hopes and dreams for the future—our feelings. These female qualities are especially strong during teen years and continue to be healthy expressions in adulthood when women become wives and mothers.

Vision and Action: See and Do

How do we begin to describe guys? They are visual creatures, driven by what they see. They love to engage in activities that require brain and brawn: sports, hiking, driving cars, ad infinitum. Men often talk about the great game they watched last night. In fact, the only thing they enjoy more than viewing a desirable activity is actually engaging as an active participant in that activity—being a quarterback in the big game or a jockey astride Sea Biscuit's back.

Their greatest delight is to combine visual and tactical skills—the seeing and the doing. The beautiful cheerleaders on the sidelines? You say, *Oh, they're just cheering the team on.* Don't kid yourself. They are, in a state of semi-dress, dancing like sugar plums in the heads of the male spectators. No man is immune, but their suggestive dances are especially provocative in the minds of guys in their teens and those in their early adulthood. In the sexual sense, the man's "seeing and doing" is a healthy expression in the marriage relationship with his

With Guys, the Eyes Have It

Homework: Observe the guys:

* A cute girl dressed in tight or skimpy clothing walks by.
* Lovely girls parade across the TV screen during a commercial.
* A cute girl in a low cut tank top walks by while you are conversing with the boys.

Here's how I feel when I observe the scenes described above:

____

____

Why do girls dress in too-revealing clothing?

____

Sacrifice. Persecution. How are these words relevant, considering the fact that God's girl will not allow the ogling that the world's girl craves?

____

____

I Don't Understand!

Why do I usually want to understand before I obey? Is this my way or God's way?

When I read about modesty in the Bible, why do I need to obey God's rules, even if I do not understand?

Thought Question: What Bible character sacrificed greatly to obey God without question, even though he did not understand? (Gen. 22)

wife, but these cheerleaders are not their wives!

What about Me?

"What do these male-female differences have to do with me?" you might be asking. Answer yourself, "I'm a female, I am responsible, and I am God's girl." Here's a major point. Instead of taking off clothes, put on some. Few girls realize what they do to a man and how vulnerable they become when they are "unclothed." Of course, all of us are aware that our clothes, or lack of clothes, have an effect on the opposite sex, but most young women cannot know the series of actions they set into motion in a young man's life when they strut before him in a state of immodest dress. Sometimes these actions continue in motion long enough to end with devastating consequences. They did for Bathsheba.

How can you girls know your effect on guys? Here's the complication: You don't understand because you don't have the experience. You shouldn't have the experience yet, because God says no to pre-marital sexual relationships. So you must trust older women like me, who try to let you in on the secret to modest behavior and dress. Trust me, trust me. We often get the answer, "Because I said so," from a parent or teacher. But older women transgress when they fail to admonish young women to be discreet, chaste, and good (Titus 2:5).

Because I Said So

Would you even be here if someone had not yanked you out of the street when you wanted to play in traffic? "Because I said so" is not limited to parents. God is the ultimate authority.

> "Because I said so" is a sufficient reason for obedience in and of itself. There is not always time for a logical discourse when your child is stepping into traffic or

My Claim to Godliness

Fill in the blanks below with your name:

____________________ . . .

adorn . . . with proper clothing, modestly and discreetly, not with braided hair and gold or pearls or costly garments, but rather by means of good works, as is proper for ____________________ (is) making a claim to godliness (1 Tim. 2:9–10 NASB).

Read the above scripture again. How does God's girl make her claim to godliness?

____

____

____

____

____

____

____

____

____

Adorned with Good Works

Interview a godly woman, asking the following questions. Record your answers to discuss in class.

1. Why is it important that I show less skin instead of more skin?

2. How does it make me "vulnerable" when I dress in too-tight, too-short, too-low clothing?

3. What is your advice to me regarding "modest" clothing?

climbing a guardrail. Ephesians 6:1 does not give a guide for rounds of affirmative and negative dialogue, after which, if the child agrees, he should obey the parents.

We are not in a position to ask God why, because our knowledge is way too limited to understand His greatness. It's like we are four. His all-knowing wisdom is so far beyond our grasp that we must accept His "because I said so" with full confidence (Celine Sparks, *Because I Said So* [Huntsville, AL: Publishing Designs, Inc., 2010], pp. 150–52).

Girls, male and female sexual responses are each unique. God made them so. And that difference does make a difference. The security of the home and its happiness are based on that difference.

Responsibility and Accountability

"Aren't men responsible for their own souls?" you might

ask. Yes. Each person, male or female, is responsible for personal choices. Each person will be accountable in the Day of Judgment, judged according to his or her own deeds (Romans 2:6). But notice what Jesus said to men:

> Whoever looks at a woman to lust for her has already committed adultery with her in his heart (Matthew 5:28).

Where is the specific counterpart of Jesus' statement to women? It doesn't exist. Does that mean women cannot commit sin by lusting after men? Of course not. But what it does say is that men and women perceive the opposite sex very differently.

Do women have any responsibility for the souls of men? Yes. Women have the ability, with their actions and attire, to cause men to sin. A very lucrative business is based on this principle—pornography. Boys whose hormones are beginning to flood their brains are especially at risk. For years

My Responsibility

How can I cause a guy to sin? (See Matthew 5:28.)

Why should I direct my questions about the opposite sex to the Bible and the church rather than to worldly peers?

Who is best qualified to help me with modesty decisions?

The average child sees their first porn by the age of 11. Between 60 and 90 per cent of under-16s have viewed hardcore online pornography, and the single largest group of internet porn consumers is reported to be children aged 12 to 17 (Psychology web site: http://www.psychologies.co.uk).

Why is pornography a problem for the "under 16s"?

Clothing Myself

All of you who were baptized into Christ have clothed yourselves with Christ (Gal. 3:27).

How can I clothe myself with Christ?

____

____

____

____

____

____

____

____

How do I "take off Jesus"?

____

____

____

____

____

their minds have been on cars and trucks, Legos, and video games. Suddenly they awaken to the beauty of the female species. They have no idea what is happening to them, but the feeling is real and they are incapable of returning to their previous days. You will forever be their desire and their focus. How's that for responsibility?

Putting Jesus On and Taking Him Off

We are clothed with Christ when we are baptized (Galatians 3:27). Keeping ourselves clothed with Him involves a daily assessment of our souls and yielding to His will in thought and action. Allowing the latest fashion trends to dictate our dress means we've simply yielded to the world. You see, as we begin to experiment with tight, revealing, provocative clothes, we begin to take off Jesus.

Let's be objective about the matter. Josie's Monday morning is just the tip of the modesty iceberg, so let's all take her challenge. When you're deciding what to put on, consider these questions:

* Wearing these clothes, will I help my Christian brothers as they try to live for Christ?
* Wearing these clothes, could I represent Jesus in my daily walk?
* Wearing these clothes, could I talk to someone about Jesus?
* Wearing these clothes, could I have a conversation with Jesus actually present?

Do not be conformed to this world, but be transformed by the renewing of your mind . . . (Rom. 12:2).

Conform means

___

___

___

Transform means

___

___

___

Girls, please protect the souls of your brothers in Christ by wearing modest clothes. Consider how your clothes affect your Christian influence. It may be tempting to look fashionable, but God has asked us not to be conformed to the world but to be transformed (Romans 12:2). Please consider how the clothing you wear affects the men you meet leisurely outside the home: at school, at work, and at play. Please consider what you wear to worship. Men serving the Lord's supper often have difficulty keeping their minds focused on spiritual matters when the women's dresses are raised half way between their knees and thighs. Sometimes those men have nowhere to look but up.

Women of all ages should wear modest clothing to worship— to any public event, as for that matter. We are called to be different because we wear the name of Christ. He has bought us with His own blood and our outward clothing should reflect that ownership (1Corinthians 6:19–20). Modesty is a vital part of right living for women and men of all ages. Young women, decide to lead souls to Jesus with a godly, modest appearance. The world will notice. Pledge this day forward to wear Him well . . . with right living, good works, and modesty.

How High Is too High and How Low Is too Low?

- Can cleavage be seen at your neckline? If so, it's too low!
- When you bend over, do you have to hold your neckline against your chest to keep someone from seeing down your blouse? If so, it's too low!
- Can your undergarments be seen at your neckline or through your armholes? If so, it's too low or your armholes are too large!
- Can your undergarments be seen through your clothing? If so, your clothing is most likely too thin, too light-colored, or too tight!
- When you bend over, does your skirt go up above your knees in the back? Does your blouse travel up exposing your back? If so, they are both too high!
- Does your blouse allow your midriff to show or does it have narrow or thin straps? If so, it's too high and too low!
- When you sit and cross your legs, does your skirt slide halfway up your thighs? If so, it's too high!
- When you sit down in a skirt with slits, is the slit above your knees? If so, it's too high!
- Is your back exposed? If so, it's too low!

—by Patsy Norwood, used by permission

People, even more than things, have to be restored, renewed, revived, reclaimed, and redeemed; never throw out anyone. Remember, if you ever need a helping hand, you'll find one at the end of each of your arms. As you grow older, you will discover that you have two hands, one for helping yourself, the other for helping others.

Audrey Hepburn, when asked to share her beauty tips, said the following:

> The beauty of a woman is not in the clothes she wears, the figure that she carries, or the way she combs her hair. The beauty of a woman must be seen from her eyes because that is the doorway to her heart, the place where love resides. The beauty of a woman is not in a facial mode. Her true beauty is reflected in her soul. It is the caring that she lovingly gives, the passion that she shows. The beauty of a woman grows with the passing years.

Beauty Tips

For attractive lips, speak words of kindness.
For lovely eyes, seek out the good in people.
For a slim figure, share your food with the hungry.
For beautiful hair, let a child run his or her fingers through it once a day.
For poise, walk with the knowledge that you never walk alone.

* Leading in Daily Devotion *

Day	Bible Reading	Self-Check
1	2 Samuel 11:1–17	Am I aware of how my clothing affects others?
2	Romans 2:6	Am I ready for God to judge my deeds?
3	Matthew 5:28	Am I a stumbling block to men?
4	Galatians 3:27	Am I clothed with Jesus, through baptism?
5	1 Timothy 2:9–10	Am I more focused on clothes or professing godliness with good works?
6	Romans 12:1–2	Am I conformed to the world or to Jesus?
7	1 Corinthians 6:19–20	Am I glorifying God with my body?

God's Girls Lead with Purity

Let no one despise your youth, but be an example to the believers in word, in conduct, in love, in spirit, in faith, in purity.

1 Timothy 4:12

In those few days before Christmas, you can know for sure that mystery was in the air after hours in our house.

"How are we going to keep Teresa out of the box until Christmas morning?" my father must have said around eleven one night. You see, at an early age I was known for peeking early. "I guess we could hide it in the trunk," Daddy teased.

"I don't think so," Mom said, "since the other children's gifts are under the tree. We don't want her to feel slighted. But you have a point. She went right into that one last year about three days early."

"Tell you what." Mom was always creative. "Why don't we put extra tape on all the sides around the box? Let's make it as hard as we can for her to get into it.

When I look through old photos, the evidence is there. I cannot suppress giggles when I see the picture of one of my mended packages under the tree with crisscrossed tape on the ends, until Mom and Dad finally figured out how to handle my curiosity.

Christmas gifts, birthday gifts, and all gifts have a certain amount of mystery. So what's in the box? If we give in to temptation and take a peek, the mystery immediately evaporates. We can rewrap it and tell no one we had a sneak peek, but we will not be able to open the gift with a sincere, genuine surprise, no matter how much we would like to please Momma and Dad. The mystery's gone, never to be restored.

Who Knows Me Best?

Pure *adj* \'pyůr\
: free from what vitiates, weakens, or pollutes
: containing nothing that does not properly belong
: free from moral fault or guilt
: marked by chastity

I know God expects me to be pure, but how do I find out specifically how to do that?

____

____

____

____

A Gift from God

A young woman's sexual purity is a precious gift from God. *Pure* means "free from what weakens or pollutes." For instance, *pure* is used to describe gold that contains no other metals—no foreign substances whatsoever. The purer the gold, the greater its value. A young woman who is sexually pure is free from that which spiritually weakens and pollutes souls.

Where do we go to find out what weakens and pollutes? Why don't we go to the one who knows the human—body and soul—more than any other? Our Creator, God, is that source.

God Knows How We Tick

God did not create us as complex human beings and leave us without direction. He gave us an owner's manual for human living, the Bible. He knows how we tick—what is good for us and what is bad. God has clearly said throughout Scripture that sex before marriage and sex outside marriage is sin.

> Marriage is honorable among all, and the bed undefiled, but fornicators and adulterers God will judge (Hebrews 13:4).

When we live according to the owner's manual, our minds and bodies function properly. More important, our souls are right with God.

Sexual purity is a gift. This special gift is to be given only at a specified time, a woman's wedding day, and only to one person, her husband. The world is literally shouting that it's acceptable—intended!—that a young woman have sexual encounters before marriage. Some teen magazines

Knitted in Mom's Womb

Write "God" in the blanks below:

For _________ formed my inward parts; _________ knitted me together in my mother's womb. I praise _________. For I am fearfully and wonderfully made . . . My frame was not hidden from _________. . . The eyes of _________ saw my unformed substance. (See Ps. 139:13–15 ESV.)

God knew about every day I would live, even before I was born. Psalm 139:16 says ". . . when as yet there was _____________________."

Fornication

Find two scripture references that will answer the question, "Is fornication a sin?"

1. ___________________________

2. ___________________________

Abstain

Go back and review "counterculture" in chapter 3. Why is it countercultural to abstain from sex before marriage?

____

____

____

____

Write the name of a movie produced in the last five years that encourages saving sex for marriage.

____

Now write the name of a movie produced in the last five years that encourages having sex before marriage.

____

Which of the above questions was easier?

____

If you love me, keep my commandments (John 14:15)

portray sex as a natural form of experimentation, essential for a good marriage. Peers often urge their Christian "friend" to abandon purity. Her boyfriend may say, "If you love me, you will . . ." But God's design for sex has always been within the safe boundary of marriage (Matthew 19:5–6).

The Game Is On

In our culture, finding a suitable marriage partner usually begins with dating, and dating ordinarily begins in the teen years. Dating experiences help a young woman find compatible traits and interests in a young man. Usually it is during the dating years that she's faced with choices that involve her sexual purity. Christian young women must lead with purity. So before dating begins, the young woman who desires purity must have a bit more than ordinary understanding of the differences in men and women.

Girls

A girl is usually guided by emotion and felt needs in her friendships, relationships, and decision-making. This is especially true as she enters the dating game. More often than not, the primary force in her relationship with a young man is emotion. If he appears to care about her, listens to her, feels her sadness and gladness, and tells her he loves her, her decision-making skills are weakened; she is vulnerable.

If You Love Me You Will

If you love me, you will. You will want me to wear clothing that is not skin tight, low cut, too short, or too revealing, because you are saving me for a time when we might begin our lives as husband and wife. You are aware that your purity of mind can be forfeited by a lustful look, so you will avoid situations in which you might be tempted to lust. You will avoid pornographic materials and places where women are usually not wearing enough clothes. You will never ask me to dance, to touch you in any impure way, or even talk to me in sexually explicit terms, because you love me and want me to walk in the light of God's love. You will never ask or expect anything of me that will cause me the pain of regret later on, but instead you will do anything to help me have a happy marriage one day. If you love me, you will.

If you love me, you will demand that our relationship has no secrets. It will be an open book, before our parents, before our friends, and before our God. You will do anything to keep it this way. You will want to make of our bodies living sacrifices, holy and acceptable. If you love me, you will (Cindy Colley, *Women of the Genesis* [Huntsville, AL: Publishing Designs, Inc., 2005], p.94).

Emotion vs. Visual Interest

Are my emotions strengths or weaknesses? Or both? Why?

Why does a guy's visual interest sometimes overrule his logic?

Companions

I am a companion of all who fear You, and of those who keep Your precepts (Ps. 119:63).

Characteriistics of my companions. (Mark your choices):

_____ 1. They wear the coolest clothes.
_____ 2. They're so loyal they'll even lie for me.
_____ 3. They fear (reverence, respect) God.
_____ 4. They have connections to the best concerts.
_____ 5. They keep God's commands.
_____ 6. They keep my grades up by giving me answers to tests.

Guys

A guy, on the other hand, thrives in activity, especially with his male peers. He thinks logically about most things, except when lured by the sight of something beautiful—at first, perhaps, a beautiful car. His visual interests also guide his decision-making process, sometimes overruling logic. At a certain point in his maturity, hormones begin to rage and his focus is set almost entirely on young women. He is totally absorbed with the new freshman girls coming to school. He gawks at each as she walks past him. He sights one that fits his visual criteria—she's pretty; she looks great in what she wears and what it exposes. The dating game begins.

A Clasp for Purity

Have you figured this out? Do you know where I'm going? I'll just drop it on you. When a teenage girl, guided by emotion, begins dating a teenage boy, guided by visual interest, that emotion-visual interest combination can be a recipe for poor decision-making. How does a young woman hold on to her purity? Perhaps this memory tool will help: CLASP. That words means holding tightly to something. As an acrostic, its letters—C-L-A-S-P—will remind you of these important actions.

C—*Choose godly friends*. Select your dates from among those friends. It is easier to maintain Christian values when you surround yourself with genuine Christians. There will be times when your faith will be tested and you will need others to guard you from evil or pull you away from sin.

L—*Listen to your parents.* Pay special attention to the dating guidelines of those who love you the most. Keep Paul's words uppermost in your mind:

> Children, obey your parents in the Lord, for this is right. "Honor your father and mother," which is the first commandment

Listen for the mention of God among your peers, facebook pages, and close friends. Are the comments respectful or disrespectful?

______

How common is "OMG" among your friends? Is it a respectful or a disrespectful term?

______

Why am I to obey and honor my parents? (Eph. 6:1–4).

1. ______
2. ______
3. ______

"I'm Outta Here!"

Why should God's girl be prepared to flee from tempting situations?

______

Why might God's girl face temptation when she's with a guy who claims to be a Christian?

______

Let no one say when he is tempted, "I am tempted by God"; for God cannot be tempted by evil, nor does He Himself tempt anyone. But each one is tempted when he is drawn away by his own desires and enticed (James 1:13–14).

Why am I tempted? Underline the answer in above scripture.

Escape!

God is faithful, who will not allow you to be tempted beyond what you are able, but with the temptation will also make the way of escape, that you may be able to bear it (1 Cor. 10:13).

What phrase in the previous scripture allows you to flee? Circle it and write it here.

____

____

True or False. Temptation is not a sin.

> with promise, "that it may be well with you and you will live long on the earth" (Ephesians 6:1–4).

Girls, listen to and obey your parents.

A—*Avoid situations that generate temptation*. Certain places make you vulnerable and you can identify them: Places where you are alone with your date, places that are dark, and places where other couples are showing too much affection. Paul spoke about these situations when he wrote to the Corinthian Christians, a people who had used sexual practices in worship of false gods:

> Flee sexual immorality. Every sin that a man does is outside the body, but he who commits sexual immorality sins against his own body (1 Corinthians 6:18).

Fornication weakens and pollutes the mind and body. A key word in Paul's warning is "flee," which reminds us of what Joseph did when Mrs. Potiphar was pursuing him.

S—*Study scriptures for strength.* Jesus used His knowledge of Scripture to battle Satan (Matthew 4:1–11). We must put the Word of God in our minds and allow it to become our helmet and sword as we battle Satan (Ephesians 6:10–20).

P—*Put pure things in your mind and heart*. Have you heard the computer expression, "garbage in, garbage out"? Actually, that expression was around for centuries before the computer age. The wise man Solomon said, "Keep your heart with all diligence, for out of it spring the issues of life" (Proverbs 4:23). What you put into your mind—books, movies, music, magazines, computers—will come out of you in words and actions.

It Is Written

Plan a "War Game" session with your Christian friends. Prepare for battle with Satan by finding Scripture to combat issues that might make you stumble.

Lying ______________________

____

Dirty Jokes ______________________

____

Disrespect ______________________

____

Fornication ______________________

____

Ridicule ______________________

____

Manipulation ______________________

____

Gifts are mysterious. Taking a peek before the official gift-opening day removes the mystery, a treasure that can never be restored. Your sexuality is a precious gift. It is a gift that God intended to be given at a specified time, your wedding day, and only to one person, your husband. Before you begin to date, understand the priceless nature of that gift, and realize your responsibility. Once given away, you will never be able to recover it. Understand the vital importance, as a Christian woman, of your leading with purity. Let CLASP become your memory tool to assist you in holding on to your sexual purity. Then on your wedding day you will be able to present your husband and God a priceless gift, the mysterious and beautiful gift of purity.

Leading in Daily Devotion

Day	Bible Reading	Self-Check
1	Psalm 139:13–16	I will appreciate my mind and body as unique creations of God.
2	Hebrews 13:4	I understand that fornication is sex outside marriage and it is sin.
3	Matthew 19:5–6	I realize the safe boundary for sex is marriage.
4	Psalm 119:63	I will surround myself with people who will help me reach heaven.
5	Ephesians 6:1–4	I will listen to my parents and be guided by their wisdom.
6	1 Corinthians 6:18	I realize the serious nature of sexual sin and I will run from it.
7	Proverbs 4:23	I will guard my mind from sin that may come to me in books, movies, music, magazines, computers, or in any other way.

God's Girls Lead with Words

He who speaks truth declares righteousness, but a false witness, deceit. There is one who speaks like the piercings of a sword, but the tongue of the wise promotes health.

Proverbs 12:17–18

"Hey, Emma!" It was Jennifer, Erica's right-hand girl, sporting her designer jeans and twirling her cool iPod. "Did you kill those rats?"

Duck and run! No, I must not. Erica and three others of the in-crowd were at their lockers waiting for the punch line, so Emma chose what she thought was the lesser of the two evils. She spoke. "I don't understand, Jennifer. What rats?"

"The ones that slept in your hair, dummy!" The Erica gang hooted; Jennifer taunted, "I don't think quarterback Todd will ever throw you another pass because you dropped that good one Friday night. You could have taken it into the end zone."

Emma was devastated. "Well, uh . . . I didn't . . ."

Erica interrupted with a soft, seemingly sympathetic voice: "Sorry, Emma. This is for your benefit. Todd called Carla Sunday night while you were at church and told her all the things he learned about your Sunday school class on your date—that's not what he called it—last Friday night. And you're still a vir—. Oh, I shouldn't have brought that up, but that's what Todd said. Don't know how he knows. Anyway, he said he would never again be seen with you because you are a 'nerdy, crossed-legs Bible thumper!' His words, sweetie, not mine. But I have to agree with him. You are a nerdy, crossed-legs Bible thumper!"

Erica's gang took up the chant: "Bible thumper, Bible thumper; she's a nerdy, crossed-legs, Bible thumper. Bible thumper, Bible thumper . . ."

Emma ran, but the nauseating sound kept ringing in her brain: "Bible thumper, Bible thumper, nerdy, crossed-legs Bible thumper; Bible thumper, Bible thumper . . ."

Emma was their newest target. It seemed they took delight in taunting her. Their unkind descriptions and put-downs were hurtful. In private at last, she stood there embarrassed, muttering under her breath. Silently she thought about the old saying: *Sticks and stones may break my bones, but words can never hurt me.* Whoever said it didn't have to go to school with these girls!

Have you ever been in Emma's situation? If so, you've learned a painful reality. People can be cruel, and the tools of their cruelty often come from their mouths. Words matter. They are used to build or to destroy, to criticize or to compliment, to complain or to offer a warm thank you, to boast about accomplishments or to confess one's sin, to curse in anger or to praise God with a joyful heart.

Forever Words

You probably hear about the dangers of drugs and alcohol in Bible classes and devotionals. But when was the last time you studied about good and bad uses of words? Without instruction, you may not think of the spiritual consequences of the words you speak, email, text, and facebook to others. Eternal punishments and rewards are tied to our words.

Maybe you've been led to believe that using bad language is normal. You may think everyone does it. After all, bad language seems to guide music and culture. Television and movies make profanity seem commonplace, even glamorous. But the reality is, bad language is not normal for God's girls. We do not talk like worldly girls. A Christian is guided in all things by Christ.

Good uses of the tongue may include complimenting others, praising God, singing spiritual songs, confessing Christ, confessing one's sin, praying, encouraging others,

Soul in the Balance

Put your name in the blanks in the following paraphrased text:

For every idle word____________ may speak, she will give account of it in the day of judgment. For by ____________ words she will be justified, and by____________ words she will be condemned. (See Matthew 12:36–37.)

Let no corrupt word proceed out of ____________ mouth, but what is good for necessary edification, that it may impart grace to the hearers. (See Ephesians 4:29.)

Define *edification*. How can edification "impart grace"?

____

____

____

____

____

____

Liars of the Bible

Therefore, putting away lying, Let each one of you speak truth with his neighbor, for we are members of one another (Eph. 4:25).

Write the names of famous Bible liars beside their quotation in the blanks below:

______________ "You will not surely die."

______________ "He raped me!"

______________ "I do not know the man."

______________ "We sold our land for this price."

List at least two other liars of the Bible:

____

____

____

____

counting blessings, telling the truth, or teaching the lost. Bad uses include complaining, grumbling, criticizing, lying, slandering, gossiping, boasting, cursing, and using profanity.

The Bible tells of those who spoke words to accomplish evil. The first to tell a lie was Satan when he deceived Adam and Eve in the garden. Jesus called him the father of liars (John 8:44).

The second liar was Cain. Lamech was a boaster. Potiphar's wife lied about Joseph, resulting in a twelve-year imprisonment. The Israelites grumbled and complained until finally God made that generation die in the wilderness. The biblical examples go on and on. Scripture also allows us to see the potential for good in the spoken word. David wanted his words to be pleasing to God:

> O Lord, you have searched me and known me . . . there is not a word on my tongue, but behold, O Lord, You know it altogether (Psalm 139:1–4).

And he said,

> Let the words of my mouth and the meditation of my heart be acceptable in your sight, O Lord, my strength and my Redeemer (Psalm 19:14).

Solomon wrote about both good and bad words. He said, "A word fitly spoken is like apples of gold in settings of silver" (Proverbs 25:11). Who can put a value on kind words spoken at the appropriate time? He wrote about talebearing and lying:

> A talebearer reveals secrets, but he who is of a faithful spirit conceals a matter (Proverbs 11:13).

> Lying lips are an abomination to the Lord, but those who deal truthfully are His delight (Proverbs 12:22).

It sounds as if Solomon had encountered a few gossips and liars.

Words originate in the mind. Jesus said, "Out of the abundance of the heart the

Words God Hates

These six things the Lord hates, yes, seven are an abomination to Him: a proud look, a lying tongue, hands that shed innocent blood, a heart that devises wicked plans, feet that are swift in running to evil, a false witness who speaks lies, and one who sows discord among brethren (Prov. 6:16–19).

Find something in the previous scripture that has to do with words God hates. Circle it.

Be Ye Kind

Add to this list of kind words:

"I forgive you."
"You are so good to me."
"Thank you."
"You're kind to include me."
"How thoughtful!"

____

____

____

____

Keep Your Word!

Let what you say be simply "Yes" or "No"; anything more than this comes from evil (Matt. 5:37 ESV).

When I make an appointment and say, "See you Tuesday at six," then fail to show up, why is it a lie?

___

___

___

You brood of vipers! How can you speak good, when you are evil? For out of the abundance of the heart the mouth speaks (Matt. 12:34 ESV).

Why was it okay for Jesus to call men "brood of vipers," but it's not okay for me to speak against Jesus?

___

___

___

mouth speaks" (Matthew 12:34). He taught about the good use of words—praying (Matthew 6:9–15); confessing Christ (Matthew 10:32); and restoring a fellow Christian (Matthew 18:15). He was touched by ones who used words to honor Him, like John (John 1:29). He used His own words, many times in parables, to teach and encourage.

Watch Your Mouth

Jesus taught about the dangers of using our mouths in a negative or sinful way—swearing (Matthew 5:34); boasting (Matthew 6:2); making false promises (Matthew 5:37). He said one day we will give an account for every idle word we've spoken (Matthew 12:36–37).

Our Lord suffered as a result of others' words. Peter denied three times that he knew Jesus, the last time with cursing (Luke 22:59–62). When Jesus heard Peter's words and looked into his eyes,

Peter was so guilt ridden he went out and wept bitterly.

The Jews accused Jesus of blasphemy. They told authorities He was a threat to Rome because He said He was able to destroy the temple and build it in three days. Their name-calling and accusations pressured Pilate to condemn Jesus to be crucified.

Paul wrote to the early church saying they should put away lying and speak truth (Ephesians 4:25). He encouraged them to let their words, as well as their actions, reflect Christ:

> And whatever you do in word or deed, do all in the name of the Lord Jesus Christ (Colossians 3:17).

My Words

If someone paid you ten cents for every kind word you said about people, and collected five cents for every unkind word, would you be rich or poor?

____

Today, I will make my words reflect Christ in the following ways:

1. ______________________________

____

____

____

____

____

2. ______________________________

____

____

____

____

____

Emma's quiet and hurried exit from the taunting girls was a proper action for a Christian lady. Later that week, on her way to lunch, she saw Erica crying in the office. Emma had missed the news that had been floating around since mid-morning: Erica's grandmother had died and she was waiting for her dad to come and take her home.

As soon as Emma learned of Erica's loss, she ran back to the office and threw her arms around her classmate.

"Erica, I'm so very sorry to hear of the death of your grandmother. I was deeply hurt by my grandmother's death last year, but even so, I still cannot know the way you feel now. But I do know it's a horrible emptiness."

"Thanks, Emma," Erica muttered through her sobs. "You are sweet to care."

"I am standing by to help. I will take careful notes in biology and share them with you. And you won't have to worry about algebra. I will bring you up to date when you are ready. Your "A" will be secure in that class."

Emma released Erica from her warm embrace. Through tearful eyes, Erica watched as Emma stepped to office door and waved good-bye, tears running down her cheeks. Only Erica—and God—knew how much Emma's Christlike attitude had touched her.

Words matter, and don't let anyone convince you otherwise. Words have the ability to harm or destroy more quickly than sticks and stones do. Young women, please use your speech to build good relationships, encourage others, and teach the lost. Let kind words, prayers, and songs of praise become the fruit of your lips. If there was ever a time when young women need to lead with good words, the time is now.

* Leading in Daily Devotion *

Day	Bible Reading	Self-Check
1	Psalm 139:1–4	Am I comfortable with the knowledge that God knows my words before I speak them?
2	Proverbs 25:11	Do I use my words to teach and encourage others?
3	Proverbs 11:13	Do I listen to slander, gossip, and unkind things about others?
4	Matthew 5:34; 6:2	Do I swear? Do I boast about accomplishments or righteous works?
5	Matthew 12:36–37	Will my words justify me in the presence of God or condemn me?
6	Ephesians 4:25	Do I speak the truth?
7	Colossians 3:17	Would Jesus put His stamp of approval on all my words?

God's Girls Lead with Service

Whoever desires to become great among you, let him be your servant. And whoever desires to be first among you, let him be your slave—just as the Son of Man did not come to be served, but to serve, and to give His life a ransom for many.

Matthew 20:26–28

"But Mom. He's my hero. I want to go to his concert!"

"Brianna, we have another appointment Wednesday night."

"I know, but I can miss Bible study just this once. We've gone every time since last summer."

"Yes, that's when we all made a commitment to put Christ first. You watched as your father and I were baptized into Christ, and then we witnessed your immersion. Life goes on, but spiritual things are in first place."

"Yes, Mom, but he's adorable."

"Brianna, I'm thankful to Jim and Ann for bringing us to Christ. We have a new outlook on life. You know, my world stopped a few years back when my young Hollywood hero died. I was about your age. I thought Hollywood was filled with gods and goddesses. I've since learned that many popular entertainers leave life early because they cannot use their wealth and popularity to bring them as much fun as they think they deserve. No, Brianna. You cannot go to the concert. We will go to Bible study."

Brianna dropped her head. "Mom, I do see the difference in the things my friends want and the things I should be wanting. I will do better. Thank you for being there for me. I understand."

"Thank you, Brianna. We've chosen the best part. Like it or not, our heroes chart the course of our paths. Since you are now a Christian, be careful who's invited into your hero circles."

Who are your heroes? Those who capture your admiration and devotion. Those people presently play a big role in who you are. I, like Brianna's mother, hope you wisely select and maintain your list of heroes.

I have a hero. He was unselfish, always a giver. He gave his mind, energy, and valuable time to others. Some of his contemporaries thought he shouldn't be doing that sort of thing. After all, he was from a royal family. He had an impressive title, but he valued people above titles. Even though his work was very important, he knew when everyone needed a rest. He was able to work alongside the lowliest people to get the job done.

Miracle Man Is God

My hero is Jesus. Not only are all His qualities past tense, they're present tense, too. He had what some might consider a monumental task—only three short years to guide twelve men to spiritual maturity. And He knew all the while that one would betray Him, one would deny Him with oaths, and all would forsake Him. Yet He continued to guide and influence these men, as well as thousands of others.

According to records left by His followers, Jesus delivered twenty sermons, shared thirty-one parables, and performed thirty-five miracles. He healed lepers, the paralyzed, and the blind. He fed thousands with one small lunch intended for a boy, cast out demons, and raised the dead. John tells us He did many other things that "if they were written one by one, I suppose that even the world itself could not contain the books that would be written" (John 21:25).

My Hero

In the corresponding text, underline four major accomplishments of Jesus.

Define *hero worship*.

Why do rock stars often receive hero worship?

How much time is involved in being a follower of our favorite musician?

Friends of the King

What kind of king were the disciples of Jesus expecting?

How did the apostles expect to be rewarded by Jesus?

He poured water into a basin and began to wash the disciples' feet, and to wipe them with the towel with which He was girded (John 13:5).

The King and His Men

Toward the end of His ministry, Jesus and the twelve met in a room for the Passover supper (John 13:1–17). Even though Jesus had told them on more than one occasion that He would be put to death, the idea never found lodging in their hearts. They believed Jesus was born to become an earthly king, that He would establish a physical kingdom in Jerusalem in the first century. They believed Jesus was to be their generation's King David. He would drive out the filthy Romans. It logically followed, at least in the minds of some apostles, that He would reward His closest friends, the apostles, and that He would especially reward His three closest friends. As His right-hand men, they would help Him rule the world.

Dirty Feet

Jesus knew their image of Him would soon be shattered. He would be arrested and crucified. He wanted to leave these men with the correct vision of His spiritual kingdom, the church. He would give them the key to leading or guiding others to Jesus.

In those days, travelers wore sandals along the same dusty roads that camels, donkeys, and other pack animals trod, so it was a common practice for a servant to wash the feet of guests as they entered a home. As Jesus and the twelve men entered the home for the Passover supper, no one volunteered to wash their feet (John 13:1–17).

Jesus rose from supper, removed His outer garment, picked up a towel, and tucked the end in His belt. He then poured water into a bowl and began to wash the disciples' feet, wiping them with the towel at His waist. He moved from one disciple to the next, and then to the next, and then to the next, that is, until He came to Peter: "Lord, are You washing my feet?"

You Don't Understand

Why was foot-washing important in Jesus' day?

____

____

____

____

Obviously Peter did not understand why Jesus was washing feet. How many times do I say to my parents or other authorities, "You just don't understand"? Ponder Jesus' answer to Peter and fill in the following blanks:

"What I am doing, you do not ____________ ______, but you will know ________ ________" (John 13:7)

Action before Talk

Jesus first acted properly; then He taught the lesson with words (Acts 1:1). How is this a pattern for me?

Summarize Matthew 25:31–40 in a short paragraph.

If you want to lead, learn to follow. If you want to succeed, learn to make others succeed.
—Author Unknown

Jesus answered,

> What I am doing you do not understand now, but you will know after this (John 13:7).

Not My Feet Only

Since Peter believed Jesus would soon be crowned king, he believed it was inappropriate for Him to take on the task of a lowly slave as He washed and dried feet, so he declared, "You shall never wash my feet."

But Jesus responded, "If I do not wash you, you have no part with Me." One can only imagine the change in Peter's facial expression. His confidence suddenly evaporated, and he quickly answered, "Lord, not my feet only, but also my hands and my head!"

Do As I Do

When the Savior had finished washing the dusty, dirty feet of twelve puzzled men, He explained why He had performed this humble, servant's act. The washing was an example:

> If I then, your Lord and Teacher, have washed your feet, you also ought to wash one another's feet (John 13:14).

The perfect example of a leader was Jesus. When we serve one another we're following in His steps.

Jesus wanted the twelve apostles to remember this example and understand that the servant spirit is critical to the spiritual development of anyone who seeks to lead or influence others for good. In fact, the way we serve others will determine how God ultimately judges us (Matthew 25:31–40). Women of the first century were constantly going about doing good. Tabitha, also called Dorcas, made clothes for poor widows (Acts 9:36–41) and later Lydia and Priscilla gave help and support to the missionary Paul (Acts 16:14–15; Romans 16:3–4).

His Own Hands

Aspire to lead a quiet life, to mind your own business, and to work with your own hands (1 Thess. 4:11).

Jesus used His own hands to serve. Why is it important to work "with my own hands"? (1 Thess. 4:12).

____

____

____

____

____

____

Here are two ways I plan to serve others this week:

1. ______________________________

____

2. ______________________________

____

Others First

You may not be able to make clothes, help missionaries, or go on mission trips, but there are countless quiet acts of service in which you may participate, either individually or as a group. Scan the list at the end of this chapter. Challenge yourself and your Christian friends to brainstorm about additional ideas.

Jesus encountered many with physical limitations. He gave sight to the blind and healed many hurting souls. Traveling into numerous cities, He mingled with the poor and the rich, debated law with the elite, told parables to those eager to know God, and exposed His disciples to every conceivable life situation. He didn't assume the role of leader and then rely on others to do the

Leading with Service

The small things you do can be a big blessing to others. Please open up your heart and reflect on these ways to serve.

1. Plan with a few friends to take food to a new mother each day for several days.
2. Send a note of encouragement to the preacher and his family.
3. Find a widow at church—a different one each week—and give her a hug.
4. Assist a teacher with a children's Bible class.
5. Pay a genuine compliment to the young women at your congregation.
6. Ask one of the older ladies to share a talent with you.
7. Find out who maintains the baptistry or prepares the Lord's supper and thank them.
8. Keep a record of baptisms and send cards to new members, welcoming them into God's family.
9. Tell a child you appreciate the way he/she listens, sings, or pays attention during worship.
10. Send a note to someone who has lost a loved one.

work. He was not afraid to get His hands dirty, quite literally. His example teaches us.

If anyone ever deserved to be served, Jesus did. He had impressive titles: Christ, Immanuel, Prince of Peace, Lord of lords. To say that His work was important is an understatement. The souls of all men and women, from the dawn of creation until the end of time, were hanging in the balance. Even though one of the twelve would betray Him, one would deny Him with oaths, and everyone would leave Him alone in His darkest hour, He continued to think first of others. He was willing to do more than serve. He was willing to give His life. He captures my admiration and devotion. My hero is Jesus.

11. Babysit for a new mother to go shopping, or watch the baby while she relaxes at home.
12. Sit with a single mother and help her with the children during worship.
13. Take flowers to a shut-in.
14. With a few young friends, visit/sing to a shut-in.
15. Plant flowers at the church building. (Be sure to ask permission first.)
16. Pray for someone and tell him/her of your prayer.
17. Make copies of your favorite poem, cartoon, or Bible verse, and send to people who need encouragement.
18. Write to your first Sunday school teacher and tell her how she influenced your life.
19. Do yard work—cut grass, rake leaves, pull weeds—for an aging member.
20. Write a daily devotional and share it with the other young ladies.
21. Go through your closet and pull out things you no longer wear and give them to the local shelter for battered women.
22. If you are especially gifted in a particular area—mathematics, for example—offer to tutor a child who is struggling in school.

Additional ideas

Day	Bible Reading	Self-Check
1	John 13:3–5	I will identify those within and without my congregation who have specific needs.
2	John 13:6–10	I will set a servant example for others.
3	James 1:27	I will find ways to serve widows and orphans.
4	Romans 16:1–2	I will find ways to give comfort to the lonely.
5	Acts 9:36–41	I will find ways to clothe the poor.
6	Matt. 25:31–40	I will find ways to minister to the hungry.
7	Ephesians 4:32	I will share the gift of kindness with those who need it.

God's Girls Lead with Purpose

CHAPTER 12

Go therefore and make disciples of all the nations, baptizing them in the name of the Father and of the Son and of the Holy Spirit, teaching them to observe all things that I have commanded you; and lo, I am with you always, even to the end of the age.

Matthew 28:19–20

"Would you tell me please, which way I ought to go from here?" The main character and the Cheshire cat in *Alice in Wonderland* are in conversation.

"That depends a good deal on where you want to get to," said the cat.

Alice replied, "I don't much care where."

"Then it doesn't matter which way you go," the cat observed.

Even though the things Alice saw were exciting, perplexing, and entertaining, she didn't know where she was going. In other words, her journey was aimless and haphazard—without purpose.

Have you ever felt like Alice? I certainly have. And I know young people often ask, "Why am I here?" Perhaps you've asked this question, too. You may have obvious short-term goals about schools, courses of study, and work. But after those are accomplished, which way do you go? It helps to identify your purpose and determine where you are going. As children of God, we know where we are going.

Look to Jesus for Purpose

Jesus left His heavenly home to come to earth. He must have had a real mission, for His decision required tremendous sacrifice. Note three reasons for His earthly tour.

* "Do not think that I came to destroy the Law or the Prophets. I did not come to destroy but to fulfill" (Matthew 5:17).
* "The Son of Man has come to seek and to save that which was lost" (Luke 19:10).
* "I have come that they may have life, and that they may have it more abundantly" (John 10:10).

Footprints of Jesus

List three aspects of Jesus' purpose.

1. ______________________________

____

2. ______________________________

____

3. ______________________________

____

Define *abundant*.

____

____

____

Fulfill the Law

Can you believe that Jesus perfectly fulfilled the law in only three years? He chose twelve ordinary men, feeding them baby bites of knowledge as He went about showing God's magnificent glory.

What He showed them made a much greater impact than what He told them. Baskets of food, blind men seeing, tax paid from a fish's mouth, delivering a woman about to be stoned—He showed His apostles what it meant to care. Then He told His followers of a new, better way of life. That's show and tell.

Jesus fulfilled His mission uttering three words from a bloodstained cross: "It is finished." What was finished? He had kept the law perfectly; He had become the fulfillment of all the sacrificial offerings and other rituals the Father had required of those under Judaism. He had been the perfect example and the perfect sacrifice. He had fulfilled the

Jesus' Method

How did Jesus "show and tell"? Give 3 examples.

1. ______________________

____

____

2. ______________________

____

____

3. ______________________

____

____

Define *fulfilled*.

____

____

____

Zacchaeus Transformed

Jesus "reframed" Zacchaeus from a hated tax collector to

____

____

Do you know someone who is lost? Jesus came to __________ and ___________ the lost.

How did Zacchaeus promise to show his transformation? (Luke 19:8).

____

____

____

____

____

law of Moses. The promised Messiah lived and died just as the prophet Isaiah had prophesied in Isaiah 53.

Seek and Save

The good news after what seemed to be the bad news of Jesus' death was, "He is risen!" Jesus showed His followers that there was a seeker and Savior. Note His words in Luke 19:9–10:

> Today salvation has come to this house, because he also is a son of Abraham; for the Son of Man has come to seek and to save that which was lost.

Those words were spoken to Zacchaeus, a hated Jewish tax collector who worked for the Roman occupiers. But Jesus saw him as a most desirable candidate for salvation.

After His resurrection, Jesus did not leave His followers clueless but promised them the Holy Spirit was coming soon as a comforter and a teacher. "Tarry in the city of Jerusalem," He commanded them, "until you are endued with power from on high" (Luke 24:49). Don't you imagine they were wondering what was going to happen?

Jesus had already charged the apostles with their purpose:

> Go therefore and make disciples of all the nations, baptizing them in the name of the Father and of the Son and of the Holy Spirit, teaching them to observe all things that I have commanded you (Matthew 28:19–20).

Have you ever witnessed a dying person's final words? You don't forget them. The apostles heard Jesus' instructions that spring day atop the Mount of Olives. Then before their very eyes their great leader ascended into heaven.

The apostles waited in Jerusalem, and their waiting was not in vain. The church was born there in miraculous magnitude. God added three thousand souls to their number on the first day. The very people who crucified Jesus

Final Words

List all the words of action in Jesus' final words to His apostles:

____

____

____

Why did the apostles wait in Jerusalem after Jesus ascended into heaven?

____

____

____

____

____

What book of the Bible tells about the birth of the church?

____

Repent! Be Baptized!

Read Acts 2.
Why did the crowd respond with the question, "What shall we do?"

Define *repent*.

Define *remission*.

What was the purpose of repentance and baptism?

If the crowd had not obeyed the directives to repent and be baptized, would they still have received the remission of sins?

were convinced by Peter's moving sermon that Jesus was indeed the Christ. "Men and brethren, what shall we do?" they plaintively inquired. Peter answered,

> Repent, and let every one of you be baptized in the name of Jesus Christ for the remission of sins (Acts 2:38).

Three thousand received his words, obeyed the gospel, and became Christians that day (Acts 2).

How did Jesus seek and save the lost? He did it as He went about His daily walk: He listened, He asked questions, He healed, He taught. He saw souls in need of a Savior and applied His saving blood to them. He loved the unlovable.

Provide Abundant Life

> I have come that they may have life, and that they may have it more abundantly (John 10:10).

When you were small, did you sing, "I just wanna be a sheep—Baa"? If you are God's girl, you are a sheep. But don't get too proud of that fact. Sheep are not the smartest contestants on Animal Planet. I recommend that you read the entire tenth chapter of John—you might get some insight about the importance of a shepherd for you, little sheep.

Here's the exciting part: Jesus is our Good Shepherd. And we are a part of His purpose. He came for smelly, silly, thick-headed sheep. We can have life. Not just life—abundant life. Wow! That's purpose. That's salvation.

My Purpose—Everlasting Life

When Jesus promised us an abundant life, did that promise include an earthly life and a heavenly life like His? Ancient Job asked a question people are still asking, "If a man dies, shall he live again?"

Do you want to be dead all over like Rover? Or do you want to live forever? Do you want a new body someday—a heavenly body? That will be the ultimate makeover!

Living Forever

How is abundant life connected to eternal life?

____

____

Consider Jesus' life. How did He have an abundant life? Or did He?

____

____

Research: Comment on heaven from these two perspectives:

1. Rest ____________________

____

2. Reward ____________________

____

My soul will exist eternally in one of which two places?

1. ____________________

2. ____________________

How do I know that my soul will live forever?

____

My Citizenship

If I am a Christian, where is my citizenship? (Phil. 3:20).

___

How does the previous verse about citizenship define my actions here in my birth country?

___

___

___

___

As a "foreigner" (God's girl) how will the "natives" (worldly citizens) view my actions and my speech?

___

___

___

___

Actually, "dead all over like Rover" is not a choice for you. The soul never dies.

Back to the abundant life. Can this be *eternal* life? With Jesus? In heaven? For me? Yes. In fact, I will fulfill Jesus' purpose by living an abundant life and receiving eternal life. So Jesus' purpose becomes my purpose—heaven.

My Purpose—to Seek and Save

Remember those last words of Jesus: Go; make disciples; baptize; teach. Are these words for you and me? Peter certainly took them seriously, and the result was three thousand baptisms on the day the church began.

> Go therefore and make disciples of all the nations, baptizing them in the name of the Father and of the Son and of the Holy Spirit, teaching them to observe all things that I have commanded you; and lo, I am with you always, even to the end of the age (Matthew 28:19–20).

These words are for you and me. Did Jesus give me a purpose? Yes, one that stretches beyond concern for myself. A purpose so different it makes me look at others in a new way.

What's my mission? "Make disciples." *Who needs me?* "All nations." *What do I tell them?* "All things Jesus commanded." *What's my reward?* "Lo, I am with you always."

But you and I were not told to wait in Jerusalem for the Holy Spirit to descend on us so we could communicate in other languages, heal the sick, and raise the dead. Then how will we accomplish our purpose?

We are not clueless, just as the apostles were not clueless. By the time they all died, the Holy Spirit had inspired them to write His instructions for, guess who? Me, a sheep. I have *The Book.*

> His divine power has given to us all things that pertain to life and godliness (2 Peter 1:3).

What about Me?

What is my mission from Jesus?

____

____

____

____

____

When I feel overwhelmed about my mission, how do I go about getting help?

____

____

____

____

____

I have _____ things that pertain to ___________ and godliness. (See 2 Peter 1:3.)

Why Am I Here?

Look up Ephesians 2:10 in your Bible. Underline it. Then write in the margin, "Why Am I Here?"

Write your name in the following blanks:
___________ *is His workmanship, created in Christ Jesus for good works, which God prepared beforehand that* ___________ *should walk in them.* (See Ephesians 2:10.)

Workmanship can mean handiwork. Who made me? _________ Who prepared a way for me to live? __________

The previous verse tells me how to walk. Explain what "walk" means.

____

How do my friends factor into my purpose?

____

____

____

Maybe I don't know exactly how to begin, but I must never doubt that the answers to my purpose are in The Book.

Begin a search on how to seek and save. Ask, ask, ask. Pray, pray, pray. Check out the Open Bible Study method of making disciples. Try Fishers of Men or some other method. When you begin to learn the Scriptures, opportunities will come. Jesus' method of "show and tell" worked for His first-century disciples. It will work for you too.

As you go about your daily routine of good works, make disciples. God planned this work for you. Walk that way.

Believe it or not, you can be responsible for making disciples just by bringing a soul to a good Bible teacher. Can you do that? Of course, you say. Then you can make disciples. Jesus commanded it, and "His commandments are not burdensome" (1 John 5:3).

On any ordinary day, we connect with store clerks, students, janitors, coffee house servers, and laundry attendants. We bump into people at school, at work, at shopping centers. In each place, we come in contact with those who do not know Jesus. At any given time someone may ask, "Which way do I go from here?" We must be ready with answers. Opportunities abound.

I Can Make Disciples

Here are two people that I want to "make disciples of" (convert to Christ) this year:

1. ____________________

2. ____________________

One Young Lady

How does a girl accomplish the two-fold purpose of heaven and soul-winning? How does she stay on track to heaven? What tools or methods does she use to teach others about Jesus? When I asked one young lady these questions, she summed it up this way:

> I have set a goal to read my Bible every day, and this in itself has opened up a whole new world for me. I never before made the time or effort, and I am sad about that. Reading God's Word reminds me of who God is and what His will is for me. I am reminded that even though I might be alone physically, God is still with me. Together, these aspects keep me on track and focused. My family has always been a constant encouragement in keeping me heaven bound. I know I can talk to them about anything, and they will give me honest answers and help me search the Bible if they are unsure.
>
> My friends have always been there to pick me up and keep me on track, especially my Christian friends. The college group gets together every Monday for a devo, Wednesdays for service, and Thursdays for singing. These nights are so uplifting. As a result, we have become like a mini church. We come to each other for help and advice, confess to each other, and hold each

> other accountable. We truly love one another. Having earthly support systems like this make such a difference to me.
>
> I try to bring Jesus and the power of prayer into conversations with friends to let them know that He makes life better for me, and He can for them, too.
>
> I want to be a light by making sure I dress modestly, engage in appropriate conversation, and refrain from getting involved in questionable activities. I do not want to give anyone a reason to question who I worship and serve. A Christian is called to live different from the world, and I have taken this to heart. I still have friends who do not believe, but they know that I will never be involved in what they do. They respect me for it. People notice when others don't follow the crowd. Teens often feel they must fit in. Standing for right is hard and often frowned upon, but it makes an impression. I think that it must start there, because if I am like everyone else in the world, why be a Christian?

This godly girl has given, in a nutshell, practical ways to fulfill her purpose. Each Christian has been given this mission—reaching heaven and sharing the good news of Jesus with others. As children of God, we know where we are going. We are not aimless. Our journey is not haphazard. We are not like Alice. Rather, we have a great purpose, a dual purpose that reaches beyond the here-and-now. It stretches into eternity because our destination is heaven.

* Leading in Daily Devotion *

Day	Bible Reading	Self-Check
1	1 Timothy 4:13	I will read my Bible daily.
2	2 Timothy 1:13	I will periodically reflect on the first principles or pattern of the gospel.
3	2 Timothy 2:15	I will seek to understand correctly—to rightly divide—the Word of God.
4	Hebrews 2:1–3	I will pay close attention to the Bible.
5	2 Timothy 2:22	I will keep myself from the desires of the flesh.
6	2 Timothy 2:24	I will be gentle with others, patient, and able to teach.
7	Matthew 28:19–20	I will speak to others about Jesus wherever I go.

God's Girls Lead with Courage

Be of good courage, and He shall strengthen your heart, all you who hope in the Lord.

Psalm 31:24

Now Jericho was securely shut up because of the children of Israel; none went out, and none came in (Joshua 6:1).

It was not that Jericho was such a large city. On the contrary, it was not. But it was well fortified: Thick walls surrounded the city and enclosed a mighty fighting force. None of the locals made attempts against Jericho. But Jericho was afraid of the God of the Israelites.

God seemed rather nonchalant about the matter:

See! I have given Jericho into your hand, its king, and the mighty men of valor (Joshua 6:2).

Israel's present leader Joshua had served as a spy forty years earlier and encouraged their fathers to go up against the Canaanites, but they had not listened. Now their graves were in the wilderness.

But this generation knew they could trust Joshua because he trusted God. They were ready to listen.

> You shall march around the city, all you men of war; you shall go all around the city once. This you shall do six days. And seven priests shall bear seven trumpets of rams' horns before the ark. But the seventh day you shall march around the city seven times, and the priests shall blow the trumpets. It shall come to pass, when they make a long blast with the ram's horn, and when you hear the sound of the trumpet, that all the people shall shout with a great shout; then the wall of the city will fall down flat. And the people shall go up every man straight before him (vv. 3–5).

Foolish instructions? Yes, from anyone except God, because God gives power to what otherwise seems foolish. God's leader didn't hesitate; neither did Israel.

When you read an amazing historical account in the Bible, do you wonder how the ancients were able to do such extraordinary things? Consider Joshua and the Israelite nation under his command. God's people were not fighters or soldiers. They were shepherds, and they had been for centuries. But they were called by God to go to battle against all the nations of Canaan, to take the land as their own. How could they do that?

The first chapter of Joshua begins with God's call to this great leader. The Lord said,

> Be strong and of good courage for to this people you shall divide as an inheritance the land which I swore to their fathers to give them. Only be strong and very courageous (Joshua 1:6–7).

Just a few sentences later He said,

> Have I not commanded you? Be strong and of good courage; do not be afraid, nor be dismayed, for the Lord your God is with you wherever you go (Joshua1:9).

Three times God told Joshua to be courageous. If he and the people obeyed the Lord's command, they would have success. In other words, if they held on to God, God would hold on to them.

Source of Strength

Joshua led the Israelites with courage. He sent spies to Jericho to scout the city and its defenses. Rahab, a woman of great courage, hid the spies. She risked her life and the lives of her family, saying,

> The Lord your God, He is God in heaven above and on earth beneath (Joshua 2:11).

Everyone saw God's tremendous power when, after the Israelites had fulfilled the divine seven-day directive with their marches around the city, God literally brought down the walls. It is evident that the source of their strength and courage was God Almighty.

The definition of *courage* is "mental or moral strength to venture, persevere, and

God Goes with Me

Be strong and of good courage, do not fear nor be afraid of them; for the Lord your God, He is the One who goes with you. He will not leave you nor forsake you (Deut. 31:6).

Remember what we learned about developing moral strength in chapter 4? Review the section "God Is Near." Now underline the section of the verse above that means "God is near." Write it here:

____

____

____

____

Lead with Obedience

Give an example of an obedient Bible character and the impact of that obedience.

What obstacles sometimes get in the way of our obedience?

Courage is not the absence of fear, but rather the judgment that something else is more important than fear.
—Ambrose Redmoon

withstand danger, fear, or difficulty." It suggests a quality that gives firm determination to achieve one's goal, unwilling to admit defeat. It enables one to endure through difficulties and keep a strong spirit. The courage of a Christian is rooted and grounded in Christ and the goal of heaven. In other words, it is not of our making but from God.

Courage to Be God's Girls

* *It takes courage to lead with obedience.* Peers may want you to do something that violates your parents' wishes. Someone may tempt you to break the law. Fellow workers may ask you to go against the wishes of your employer. College classmates may try to influence you to violate school rules or God's rule of conduct. It takes courage to obey. But God's girls understand that obeying God includes obeying all authority figures.

✻ *It takes courage to lead with love.* The vast majority of people will be kind to you if you are kind to them. On the other hand, you have likely met beasts who are difficult to love. Unless you are a hermit on an uncharted island, you will encounter more. The unlovable ones may be few, but they seem like a pebble in the shoe, either a constant irritation or an outright pain. Courage will lead you to love them anyway.

✻ *It takes courage to lead with good character and decency.* The world is telling you that dishonesty is normal. Your classmates or associates may ask you to lie or cheat. You may rarely hear expressions of gratitude from your friends or fellow workers. Those who do not practice self-control are usually applauded and emulated. That is the world in which we live. You will need courage to rise above these

Lead with Love

When people are unlovable, I need to _________ them anyway.

What chapter in the Bible defines love in word and deed?

____

Lead with Character and Decency

Why do people often laugh and accept liars and cheaters?

____

____

____

____

____

____

Courage is doing what you're afraid to do. There can be no courage unless you're scared (Eddie Rickenbacker, *Bits & Pieces*, April 29, 1993, p. 2).

Lead with a Positive Attitude

Why is it easier to focus on a person's weakness, rather than her strengths?

____

____

____

____

Whatever you do, you need courage. Whatever course you decide upon, there is always someone to tell you that you are wrong. There are always difficulties arising that tempt you to believe your critics are right. To map out a course of action and follow it to an end requires some of the same courage that a soldier needs. Peace has its victories, but it takes brave men and women to win them.
—Ralph Waldo Emerson

things and become a person of character and decency.

* *It takes courage to lead others with a positive attitude.* You will have anxious moments and possibly worry and fret because of them. It takes courage to endure difficult times and see the potential for good, even in adversity. You will likely be tempted to focus on the weaknesses of others. And some will grumble and complain, rather than use their energy to bring about positive change. God's girl of courage will trust Him in each situation, try to see the good in others, and encourage them to feel good about themselves.

* *It takes courage to be content in a world that embraces materialism*. Perhaps we become uncomfortable when our friends have everything money can buy, and when those same friends pressure us to purchase the newest gadget or the coolest car. Advertising may make you

feel as if you deserve these things and more. But despite what others may think, courageous young ladies will not conform to materialistic pressure.

* *It takes courage to be humble when you live in a society that glorifies pride*. It is not easy to be humble when those around you seem to get ahead by boasting about their accomplishments and credentials. Though the world may not understand, a courageous young lady has a heart filled with humility.
* *It takes courage to be modest and reflect Jesus in your appearance.* The world wants you to purchase and wear seducing clothes. Some of your friends are stylish. They wear the latest scanty fashion. But God's girl of courage will let Jesus guide her appearance as well as every other aspect of life.
* *It takes courage to remain pure when you live in a world that glorifies sex before marriage,*

Lead with Contentment

Why is "more" often less?

____

____

Be strong and very courageous, that you may observe to do according to all the law which Moses My servant commanded you; do not turn from it to the right hand or to the left, that you may prosper wherever you go (Josh. 1:7).

Circle "from it" in the above verse. What was "it"?

____

How can we prosper wherever we go?

____

____

Lead in Modesty

What does God's girl wear? (Circle one.)

The latest scanty fashion

Good works

Lead with Purity

When I am with non-Christians, how can I have the courage to be a part of their counterculture?

What is one scripture that tells me to be pure?

Lead with Words

What will ultimately judge me?

Courage doesn't always roar. Sometimes courage is the little voice at the end of the day that says "I'll try again tomorrow."
—Mary Anne Radmacher

Lead with Service

Priscilla and Aquila, my fellow workers in Christ Jesus . . . risked their own necks for my life . . . (Rom. 16:3–4).

How do we know that Priscilla and Aquila loved Paul?

---

or having a "live in" to see if you are compatible. Your peers may ridicule your desire to remain pure. They may scoff at the notion of virginity. But the courageous young woman will guard and cherish her gift of purity.

* *It takes courage to speak as Christ would speak.* The world may bombard you with irreverent talk, crude jokes, and profanity. The people you associate with or work with may engage in words of complaint, criticism, backbiting, gossip, or slander. But the courageous girl will use words that build others up and reflect Jesus.
* *It takes courage to serve the Lord and to serve others* when you live, work, and play with those who seek only to serve themselves. But a courageous young lady will seek to serve any person in need.
* *It takes courage to remain focused on heaven*, especially when everyone and everything seem to draw

your attention away from the goal.

* *It takes courage to begin teaching others about Jesus.* But the courageous Christian young woman knows this is the great purpose given to every child of God.

Lead with Purpose

This world is not my home, my citizenship is in ______________________.

Jesus left me with a purpose of making disciples. How do I accomplish that purpose?

____

____

Courage, Obedience, Victory

New Testament Christians gave powerful examples of courage in the face of adversity and persecution (Acts 7, Romans 16:3–4). Old Testament characters like Joshua possessed courage in the face of insurmountable odds. It equipped them to lead, guide, conduct, and influence others for good. Joshua obeyed God's command, "Be of good courage," and he trusted in God's promises. The people of God followed his lead. They were courageous, and God was with them in victory. That is the reason they were able to do extraordinary things.

You need courage too. Struggles and temptations abound. The Christian walk is seldom an easy stroll. Do you have courage? Do you have firm determination to achieve your goal? Are you unwilling to admit defeat? Do you have courage to endure difficulties and keep a strong spirit? Do you trust in God's promises? Are you willing to inspire others to live for Jesus and encourage them along the way?

If you are a child of God, you have been called to walk in Christ. You possess great strength because you are rooted and grounded in Jesus. If you continue to obey and serve Him with courage, He can accomplish wonderful things through your life. I believe you are up to the great challenge of leading or influencing others toward the goal of heaven, the eternal victory. Remember, God will never leave you, nor forsake you. If you hold on to Him, He will hold on to you.

* Leading in Daily Devotion *

Day	Bible Reading	Self-Check
1	Deuteronomy 31:1–6	I know God will not leave me or forsake me.
2	Joshua 1:1–6	I will trust in God's promises.
3	Joshua 1:7	I will courageously obey God.
4	Joshua 1:8–9	I will study God's word, let it lead me in obedience.
5	Joshua 23:4–6	I will not turn aside from God's word to the left or right.
6	1 Chronicles 19:12–13	I will encourage brothers and sisters, and ask them to encourage me.
7	Acts 28:11–15	I will remember the courage of early Christians.